Chris McCubbins: Running the Distance

CHRIS McCUBBINS
RUNNING THE DISTANCE

Joe Mackintosh

J. GORDON SHILLINGFORD
PUBLISHING INC

Chris McCubbins: Running the Distance
First published 2013 by J. Gordon Shillingford Publishing Inc.
©2013, Joe Mackintosh

Cover and interior design by Relish New Brand Experience
Printed and bound in Canada on 100% post-consumer recycled paper

We acknowledge the financial support of the Manitoba Arts Council and The Canada Council for the Arts for our publishing program.

LIBRARY AND ARCHIVES CANADA CATALOGUING IN PUBLICATION

Mackintosh, Joe, 1941-, author
    Chris McCubbins : running the distance / Joe Mackintosh.

Includes bibliographical references and index.
ISBN 978-1-897289-94-5 (pbk.)

        1. McCubbins, Chris, 1945-2009. 2. Long-distance runners--Canada--Biography. I. Title.

GV1061.15.M43M32 2013   796.42092   C2013-903310-6

To Carole

Table of Contents

Preface 9
Race Face 11
Race Ready 13
The Making of a Runner 17
McCubbins Heritage 29
Snider Family Heritage 34
1967: Chris' Great Running Adventure 38
September '67—Back to OSU 50
Called for Duty 54
Modern Pentathlon 57
Back on Track 64
Olympian Dreams 70
1976 Olympics Year 83
Post Olympics 95
Sue Jacobsen 100
Sue and Chris 102
The Masters Runner 112
Chris the Coach 118
Sue Recalls the 1990 Travel Adventure 121
Back in the Classroom 123
Jack Daniels Retests for Fitness 125
One More Run 127
Last Words 139
Appendix 1: A Sample of Races 142
Appendix 2: Records 158
Sources of Information 159
Acknowledgements 164
Index 165

Preface

IN THE SUMMER OF 2009, WHILE CORRESPONDING WITH CHRIS, I RAISED the possibility of writing his biography.

> I was thinking the other day of your story and how interesting it is. You provide the information. I'll do the writing. It's time to sort out that box of yellowed news clips.

Chris replied

> Your offer is very thoughtful and touching. I do not know if at this time I have the energy or memories to help put something together. I have never thought of my life as very interesting, only charmed. I have been blessed to bounce back from and grow stronger and happier after all the previous falls. This one seems a little more difficult to rebound from.

If Chris' life wasn't interesting and worthy of remembering, whose was? He was: an All-American college track star in the 3000-metre steeple-chase, a gold medalist in the 1967 Pan American Games, a member of the elite United States Military Modern Pentathlon Team, a native record holder in Manitoba for his 28:16.51 feat in the 10,000-metre race—a record that still stands in early 2013, a Canadian Olympic athlete, an accomplished cross country skier and coach, a role model in the realm of early childhood education and looming above it all, a decent and caring human who was beyond modest about his many accomplishments. American track coach Jack Daniels once referred to Chris as the fittest-50 year-old on the planet.

I sorted through that box of tinted, tattered pieces. Here's the story.

Race Face

Anxious runners merge at the start line,
Coping with race-start jitters—
And there's Chris,
Tall in racing crowds,
Engrossed in his world,
Summoning the spirits of endurance,
Piercing opponents with
Track-warrior arrows from
Lenses of steely blue—
Hammer ready,
Confident,
Calm,
Joyful,
Race face in place.

Race Ready

CHRIS HAD A COMPETITIVE ZEAL AT THE START OF A RACE. COMPETITORS knew that he was in another space. His eyes were looking at you but not seeing you—focused solely on the race. In that zone, his face told all with such intensity; all his powers concentrated on the occasion at hand.

To enter this race-ready mode, Chris would focus on specific parts of his body. He would concentrate on his ankles because he knew that if he flicked his ankles, he would get an extra foot of propulsion. Or, he might concentrate on lifting his knees—another source of acceleration. Whatever it was, focusing helped him to concentrate on the mission of winning the race.

Once in the contest, his mental toughness, honed over a lifetime of races, predominated. Runner Dianne Sproll once asked Chris to teach her how to be tough in a race—tough enough to overcome the inevitable pain of running.

> If something—some part of your body—hurts and you are in serious pain—then think of some part of your body that feels good. Ignore the pain. Pick out a spot—a fleck or something on the jersey of the runner in front of you and focus on that. It will take your mind off the pain. You can always find something to feel good about.

Chris loved to get as much out of his body as he could—day in day out, no complaints. He never showed weakness. After arduous interval training, some runners might sit down or lean over, admitting to their pain and exhaustion. For Chris, this didn't happen. He showed little vulnerability, at most bending over to re-tie his shoes. It was like, "Look, I'm not even breathing hard"—a part of his mental game, a game he surely perfected.

A long-time friend and running colleague, Sheldon Reynolds, described how Chris was always working on sharpening the mental side.

> He loved to challenge himself—psychologically—improving his head game. We would be running up to the top of the hill and the natural tendency was to back off because you had made it to the top. Not Chris, he would keep giving it for a few more steps—widening the lead. He would run hard over the crest of the hill and then push for two strides—always trying to push farther than you think you can.
>
> Then he would say "let's go hard to the next marker"—perhaps a pole. When you got to the pole, he would say— "the next one." He knew that the mind was the key. I was too young at that time to appreciate what he was trying to accomplish. Now I understand what he was doing. I had no idea then. Chris was proving that you had more—and only your mind was the limiting factor—he realized that very early.
>
> Also, there were never any excuses. I remember coming home from a race. I would say to Chris, I knew that I could have run a better race. And he would say, "No you couldn't. If you didn't do it, you didn't do it." There was a finality to it—which is the exact opposite of many runners when there is always an excuse. Chris was so principled.

Chris didn't like to lose races and he often needed someone to prod him to trigger that competitive zeal. Friend and fellow runner Greg Gemmell explained it this way.

> One summer in the Gimli 10-mile run, it appeared that no one was up to pushing him. So just after the start he looked back at me and motioned to "C'mon, let's go" It was a cold, rainy and miserable day so we ran the first five miles together. I felt real good since I was keeping pace with him. And then, at probably the beginning of the sixth mile he started to pull away. At first, he was only several

feet in front and then it increased to 10 to 15 yards—with the gap getting increasingly larger. At about the seventh-mile mark, he was out of sight. Chris had a low 48-minute run that day and I finished in the 50-minute area. I had the best run ever but it wouldn't have happened if Chris hadn't had me push.

Chris was also able to overcome bad races. He would mentally list the things that went well—perhaps the pace or lack of pain from a past injury. His advice was always to discard the negatives and concentrate on the cycle of positives.

This was why Chris was a good coach. He boosted confidence. He brought people to the point where they believed in themselves. He inspired them to run. His eyes would pierce you but he was always calm and on an even keel—methodical and analytical.

Runners often focused on the pain of running. Chris focused on the joy of running and the happiness derived from it.

For those who knew him, Chris was an icon of fitness. Thus, his diagnosis of serious health problems in February 2009 was hard to believe. It was only a year earlier that Chris was honoured by Manitoba Runners' Association (MRA)—enjoying an evening of good fun during his induction into the MRA's Hall of Fame.

CHRIS, JUNE 7, 2009

You can imagine what a shock learning I had leukemia was to Sue and me.

We were in Victoria in late November last year [2008] visiting Sue's parents. I came down with a laryngitis that put me in bed for 3 days and several days of recovery.

I seemed to get a little better for a while but then seemed to be tired all the time especially when exercising. I could not keep close when Sue and I would go for a ski. I finally went to my family doctor in early February. He took some blood tests and when he met with us he told us my blood values were really off and I was to stop exercising immediately and either he would get me an appointment with a specialist very quickly or send me to emergency to get a full work-up.

I had blood work done on Feb. 12 and saw a specialist at St. Boniface Hospital on Friday Feb 13. He did a bone marrow biopsy and told us later that afternoon that I had acute myelogenous leukemia.

I checked into Health Sciences Centre, Ward GD6, on Tuesday Feb. 16 and began my first round of chemo on Friday Feb. 20, Sue's birthday. During that treatment period I caught pneumonia which the hospital had difficulty controlling as they could not get an accurate typing. By the time it was over I had gone through a bronchoscope from which nothing was learned but it did help loosen up the crud in my lungs. I ended up losing 20 pounds during that time.

SUE, JUNE 2010

I noticed that Chris was having trouble swimming. He just couldn't get his breathing right. In July, 2008, he went for a check-up and blood tests and everything appeared normal. In November while visiting my parents in Victoria, he appeared to catch a virus and only got up for the bathroom and to eat for three days. He couldn't walk. I was really worried—they tested him for strep throat but that test was negative. It was diagnosed as just a virus. He started to recover but very slowly. We didn't think that much about it because we thought he had a bad virus. He got better—a little—but then was getting worse again. When we got home we were still going swimming and running. Even though he was getting worse, Chris kept denying it. Finally he went to his family physician in late January—and the results came in when we were skiing at Birds Hill. We didn't get back until the following week. His doctor said the white blood cells were low and hemoglobin was 80, so he sent Chris to a blood specialist in oncology at the St. Boniface Hospital to do all the tests at once. Chris' own doctor said no exercise, so that meant that Chris couldn't follow through with the Level III CANSI course—the high-level certification for cross-country ski trainers.

It took a lot for Chris to cry but I saw a tear running down his cheek. I assumed that the medical news was just too much for one day. Typical Chris, it turned out that he was most saddened by the fact he was out of the CANSI program.

The Making of a Runner

CHRIS WAS BORN ON NOVEMBER 22, 1945 IN ENID, OKLAHOMA.
Enid gained its notoriety as a cattle town in the 1870's. It was an Oklahoma stopping point for longhorn cattle and the cowboys accompanying them on the long journey from Texas to Abilene, Kansas. It was made long by the fact that the cattle would only travel some 10 miles per day before stopping for the night in order to maintain their weight and health. In addition to the cattle, there was a trail boss, some 10 to 14 cowboys, a cook and wagon, and a wrangler for the 100 to 150 horses. The prices of cattle on the east coast of the United States relative to Texas prices made the journey a profitable venture.

Enid was an ideal stopping point—an oasis of grass and water, ideal for an eating and resting point for the herds. The cattle route was known as the Chisholm Trail and was considered to be one of the wonders of the Western world. Although the trail herds averaged 2500 to 3000 head, some herds as large as 10,000 were driven up to the Abilene rail yards. From there they would be shipped to Chicago and the eastern coast of the United States.

As a youngster, Chris was a skinny kid slow in physical development and not much interested in organized sports. Instead, he liked to hang out at the "weed patch" with the rest of the kids. This was a natural play area in Enid close to his home at 405 West Market Street. There were lots of open spaces with wild grasses and plenty of trees to climb. There was a big old abandoned house on the lot where fire had left only a foundation and a basement. There was also a large culvert. He and his best friend Vic Fulton would meet there. They would crawl Marine-like through the old culvert: sliding through the cool concrete, running back through grassy trails, then clambering down the steps and into the basement. Chris' sister Rilla recalled a year when cousins stayed with them for three months. It was the best time ever. Sometimes all six of them—the three cousins, Chris, Rilla and brother Tip—would play away their days at the weed patch.

Mother Juanita described those early years.

Chris was sickly until he got his tonsils out—just pre- kindergarten. He made so much noise breathing with his adenoids and tonsils. He was so little but he had good medical help with Hope and George (Chris' aunt and uncle, Dr. Hope Snider Ross and Dr. George Ross). Then he started growing and feeling better. He was always a puny guy going through high school. One day he came home for lunch. We lived about a block from the school. He was so happy.

"Ulla Jean is back," said Chris.

"O," I said, "do you like Ulla Jean?"

"No, I don't like her—I don't like her at all—it's just that she's littler than me."

Chris, true to his life-long character and his experiences with physical activity, took some time to ponder the running decision. He was in his junior year in high school—Grade 11 in Canada—when he finally got started. It was the autumn of 1961. Fifteen years of age and dressed in blue jeans, Chris started his daily runs. It was a tentative beginning. He wanted to be sure that this was a sport he could do. His past forays into team sports hadn't worked. Being small and somewhat uncoordinated, he was often the last picked for sand-lot teams. He was a no-hitter in five years of Little League Baseball. He decided to run first in the ditches, out of sight of neighbours who might be inclined to sic their dogs on suspicious runners. Fortunately, his brother Tip was running for the high school cross country team; he saw Chris running in the trenches and coaxed him out, encouraging him instead to join the high school cross country workouts.

Tip was in his senior year in high school. He was an all-state basketball star and an accomplished performer on the track—a natural athlete.

Up to his junior year in high school, Chris was very much over-shadowed by his brother's athletic accomplishments. Tip was two years older than Chris but only one grade ahead. Chris, born in late November of 1945, started first grade at Enid's Jefferson Elementary School in 1951. He just met the age requirement by five days, turning six just prior to the December 1 cut-off date. He was only five years old for the first three months of the school year—the youngest kid in the class. His parents tried to hold him back but were unsuccessful. School authorities wouldn't bend the rules. Mom and Dad would be breaking the law if they acted on their own and they were surely law-abiding citizens.

In retrospect, it appears that Chris' mom had the correct take on the emerging runner. "Chris was practising alone in the ditches to ensure that he was good enough to come out for the high school team."

He didn't want to show up for the team and be turned down. When he finally went out, the coach "ate him out for not coming out before."

There wasn't any doubt that Chris was good enough. He surely was. He was also having fun. Running was enjoyable. It suited his quiet, introspective character. In his junior year in high school, Chris was entered in the one-mile AA regional meet. The best time, 4:34, was posted by runner Richard Cable. The first three-placed runners were invited to the state meet but Chris didn't make the cut in the mile. Later, at the meet of champions, Cable won again with a time of 4:21. Two future running mates at Oklahoma State University also ran well. Jim Metcalf ran second at 4:25 and Ray Smith was third.

Chris improved in his senior year of high school. His fastest mile time was 4:24.2, but still short of the times of his colleagues Cable, Metcalf and Smith. In addition, Chris finished 33rd in the state high school cross country meet. As a result of their high school running achievements, Smith and Metcalf received full scholarships to attend Oklahoma State University (OSU). Coach Ralph Higgins could only offer Chris financial compensation of books and tuition for his freshman year, something for which Chris was forever grateful. He was just happy to be on the College track team. He had found something he was good at.

Chris enrolled in Arts at OSU in Stillwater, Oklahoma in the fall of 1963, and 62-year-old coach Ralph Higgins was happy to have him on the team. Coach Higgins was a former student at OSU, graduating in 1925. A superb athlete, he had competed in football, basketball and track, winning the Southwest Conference 100-yard and 440-yard titles in the latter sport. Ralph Higgins became OSU's head track coach in 1935 and his teams were famous for winning titles. His 1954 cross country team won the national collegiate title. He also served as an assistant coach on the US Olympic Team staff in 1956 and 1960. He coached Jim Mashburn, a gold medalist at the 1956 Olympic Games.

The OSU running team was known as the Cowboys but often shortened in press articles to "Pokes." OSU competed in the Big Eight Conference along with Kansas University, Colorado University, Kansas State, Nebraska, Iowa State, Missouri University and Oklahoma City University. Both brother Tip and Chris were on the cross country running team.

As a freshman runner, Chris soon assumed a leadership role. He was an integral part of the OSU cross country team, competed in the one-mile, two-mile and three-mile races and assisted when called upon in relay events. On October 3, 1964, Chris ran in the Cross Country Jamboree at the Hillcrest site in Stillwater. He placed fifth of 49 runners with a time of 14:59 over this three-mile course. One month later, on November 7, Chris ran in the Big Eight Cross Country Conference Meet in Manhattan Kansas, another three-mile course. He placed seventh of 54 runners with a time of 14:43.

In his freshman year at College, 1963-64, Chris was ranked as the number one cross country runner. In addition, his best one-mile time was 4:17. Coach Higgins provided a full scholarship at the beginning of his sophomore year.

With his modesty and unassuming approach to his accomplishments, Chris would never have made reference to the fact that he was younger than his running mates. But, the reality is that if he had started school a year later, perhaps when he should have, outcomes would have been different. As a 4:17 miler in high school, it was likely that he would have had full scholarship offers from everywhere. A 4:17 mile was outstanding in high school at that time.

OSU running mate Jim Metcalf agrees.

In his frosh year, I ran a mile against Chris and he beat me a step and ran 4:17...which means that had he started school when he should have, he would have been a senior in high school the next year, and would have broken the state mile record by more than 4 seconds

And he would have been a senior in college in 1968 rather than 1967...who knows what he would have done in cross country, the 5000, 10,000 and steeplechase with an extra year—when you mature slowly like Chris did, every year makes a big difference...and there is a year where you make a big jump...

Metcalf was also impressed with Chris' training regime, his quiet confidence and his unique style.

Chris was a training demon in college...two sessions a day all year no matter what the weather...and killer interval workouts...

You could always spot him at a meet as he always wore an orange and black stocking cap...and he had braces, and he always had a toothpick slipped between the braces on the upper right and sticking out his mouth...those two things were his trademark...he was not cocky in any way...it was just Chris...

Some of the best races of his college career were yet to come. On November 22, 1965, Chris was running in the 27th National Collegiate Cross Country Championships. It was his birthday and the first year that the race was run over a six-mile course in Lawrence, Kansas, the cross country site for Kansas University. John Lawson from the University of Kansas won the race with a time of 29:24. It wasn't the only time that Lawson and McCubbins would go head to head in a race. Chris was fifth in the field of 152 runners and finished the race with a time of 30:07. Chris, who placed in the top 15 runners, qualified for the 1965 All American Cross Country Team. This was one happy birthday. The *Enid Daily Eagle* (Tuesday, November 23, 1965) ran an article on the race and Chris' win.

Chris McCubbins, Enid's "iron-man" distance runner, placed fifth in the 27th NCAA Cross Country Championships at Lawrence, Kansas, Monday and was named to the All-American Cross Country team.

But the way he did it might be considered even more amazing.

McCubbins had been doing a handstand on some parallel bars Monday morning and fell off, hurting his back. His mother, Mrs. Juanita McCubbins, said he could hardly get around for a little while, but evidently it didn't bother his running later in the day as he finished fifth in a field of 152 competitors.

McCubbins was a star miler and half-miler for Enid High School three years ago.

From the *Enid Morning News* of Sunday February 6, 1966, OSU head track coach Ralph Higgins referred to Chris as "the greatest two-miler ever in Oklahoma." Chris was still running one mile races but he was trying the two-mile. He was also running with the relay team and competing in cross country runs. He loved to run and was looking for an event—a niche race—that would fit his running attributes and style. In the spring of 1966, he was about to find it.

ON FEBRUARY 26, 1966 AT THE BIG EIGHT INDOOR CHAMPIONSHIPS IN Kansas City, Missouri, Chris ran a great two-mile race against Kansas star runner John Lawson. Chris' time was 9:12.9 and Lawson came in at 9:08.5. Lawson had also won the one-mile race that night with a time of 4:04.8.

The *Topeka Capital Journal* of Sunday, February 27, 1966 had the following take on the two-mile event:

He [Lawson] seemed to have more difficulty in the two-mile as Chris McCubbins of Oklahoma State jumped him on the 19th lap of the 24-lap race. But, Lawson stayed close and wrested the lead away with two laps to go and won by about 20 yards.

Chris was not a permanent member of OSU relay teams but in his junior year appeared as one of Coach Higgins' alternates. The task must have been somewhat daunting to Chris. The relay team had a great reputation in the Big Eight Conference especially in the 1964-65 year. Jim Metcalf, Tom Von Ruden, and John and David Perry set the world record for the two-mile relay at 7.18.3 in that year. Metcalf reminded me that David Perry, a 1:47 880 runner, was sick with strep throat and ran 1:51 in this record breaking race. If he had been healthy, "we would have broken the record by 4-5 seconds." In addition, their races that year were run on cinder tracks—volcanic ash in Fresno, California—and it was estimated that "it would take two seconds off your time to run on the composition tracks which came in, in 1968." So Chris was following impressive tracks.

The OSU team had placed first in both the two-mile and four-mile relays at Fayetteville, Arkansas on March 26, 1966. Friend and running mate Tom Von Ruden ran in the anchor position for both of these races and Chris ran in second position for the two-mile and third position for the four-mile. On April 1, 1966, the OSU team was entered in the 39th Annual Texas Relays in Austin. The race was the 2.5-mile distance medley. Jim Metcalf was running the first 440 yards (47.3) and John Perry ran second position for the next 880 yards (1:49.8). The coach moved Von Ruden to third position running 1320 yards (2:56.5). Chris was moved to run in fourth position for the closing mile.

Prior to the race, Jay Simon, the sports editor at the *Daily Oklahoman* wrote:

> The Cowboys [OSU track team] can match any team in the league for three carries, but whether McCubbins can hold off such milers as Lawson, Nightingale and Abilene Christian's Charlie Christmas is problematical.

Chris ran his mile at 4:14.6. The OSU team broke their school record in this race by a full second with a total time of 9:48.2. Unfortunately, the team placed fifth. Simon's prediction was right. There were some strong milers competing against Chris. After the race Simon wrote:

> The distance medley was almost as much of a disappointment for the Cowboys, who also led by 15 yards after three stout carries by Perry, Metcalf and Von Ruden.

Then the big gun milers took over and Chris McCubbins could not keep pace as he churned home in 4:14.6 for fifth place. At that, the Cowboys broke their school record by a full second while clocking 9:48.2.

Charlie Christmas ran the best mile of his life—4:01.2—to bring Abilene home in 9:36.5, just a second and a half above the world record.

Some 46 years later, Charles Christmas has vivid recollections of the race.

Ah yes, the distance medley at Texas Relays in 1966. I remember it quite well. Yes, it was a great race.

I was not a seasoned miler at the time, and had only run one or two miles before. However, I had heard that John Lawson of Kansas had run a 4:03 mile indoors a few weeks before the Austin event. That meant that I wanted to get far away from him. So that was my strategy.

Ken Knapp of ACU ran 47.2 on leadoff leg. Bruce Johnson ran the half in 1:50.9, Al Von Troba ran the 1320 in 2:57.5, and I ran the mile in 4:01.0. Perhaps I could have run a little faster, but ACU had the finish line in the middle of the track and Texas had the finish almost at the end of the straightaway.

Suffice it to say that I somewhat misjudged the finish line that night, and kicked a little too early, which resulted in a massive tie-up.

The world record at the time was 9:33 and change. We ran 9:36.6 I believe, if my math is correct.

Here is how the race went. I got the baton in the lead. Maybe OSU was second. Or maybe you guys [OSU] were in the lead at the exchange. I don't remember.

So I took off, who knows how fast? Anyway my first lap was 56, to get away from Lawson. Fortunately for me no one called out my split. If they had, I may have stopped!!

So then I eased up some and went through the half in 1:58. That split I heard, and then the announcer got all excited because Texas stadium had never had a sub-4-minute mile. He then got the crowd into it all, and I responded with a 60 for the third lap, which gave me a 2:58 at the 1320, and I was feeling great.

Lawson was nowhere in sight. I wanted my Texas Relays Omega wristwatch. So I ended up with a 4:01 even with tying up on last part of the the extra long straightaway. It was a blast. I will always remember it with fond memories.

I think Kansas took second place. It was a blessing for me that Jim Ryun was a freshman, and could not run on the Kansas varsity. I had another 4:01 later at Drake in the four mile relay. This time Kansas won as our Wayne Badgley ran a "marvellous 4:23." I got the baton about half a lap behind Lawson, caught him and passed him on the backstretch of the last lap of the race, but could not hold him off later as I was pretty well spent in the early part of the race.

Perhaps the message for Chris was "I'm a better runner at the longer distances" if he was looking for a competitive advantage and a niche race. But this didn't stop him from running the mile. He still had lots to prove and he did it on his home turf at the Lewis Stadium Oval in Stillwater in early May of 1966. This was the 52nd annual dual meet between Oklahoma State University and University of Oklahoma. He came first in the one-mile race with a time of 4:20.3. Then he ran the three-mile race in a time of 14:30.8, setting both a new track record and meet record for this race.

On May 13, 1966, Chris was at the Big Eight Track Championship in Columbia, Missouri. Coming in first, he set a new record for the three-mile race with a time of 14:03.9. The old record was held by his Kansas running nemesis, John Lawson, who set the best time in the 1965 race.

Asked about Chris' success in running, sister Rilla had no difficulty isolating the key factor:

The main thing I remember is breakfast on race days...eggs, a steak, half a dozen pieces of toast, a quart of orange juice, and a half gallon of milk.

The amount Chris could eat at one sitting was something that amazed his friends throughout his life. It was a characteristic he was known for. Brother Tip was his only equal in this regard. College running mate, Tom Von Ruden had fond recollections of Chris' appetite:

> On a college break, Chris and I went back to my home near Santa Monica. My mom grew up in North Dakota so she was used to making homemade jams. This day she had a new jar on the table, maybe some 12 or 14 ounces. We had this big bacon and eggs breakfast and then Chris got into the jam. He almost finished off the whole jar himself. He piled on so much on a piece of toast that I was amazed that it wasn't falling off. I was looking at him and thinking about the amount of calories he was putting away but understood that his metabolism was very efficient and fast burning—so there was never any weight gain.

Years later, his Canadian running mates recalled a record-breaking night in Winnipeg. A local pizza restaurant had an all-you-can-eat promotion. Chris consumed 36 pieces of pizza.

Later in the fall of 1966, Chris returned again to his first love in running—the cross country race. The first race took place on October 1, 1966 on the old golf course north of the OSU Stillwater campus. It was the four-mile Hillcrest cross country course. Chris placed second in a field of 36 with a time of 19:34. Then at the Iowa State Big Eight Conference Cross Country Meet at Ames, Iowa, Chris had one of his best runs. He ran the three-mile course in 14:16.9 and placed first in a field of 52 runners. Chris' time broke the old course standard of 14:53 set in 1962 by Mike Fleming of Nebraska. McCubbins finished 23 seconds in front of the runner-up, Conrad Nightingale of Kansas State, who along with others of the top seven finishers also broke the old Fleming record. Chris had the following segment times for the race: 1/2 mile 2:11; 1 mile 4:44; 1.5 miles 7:05; 2 miles 9:40.5; 2.5 miles 11:57; 3 miles 14:16.9.

After this race, Chris received an official congratulatory letter from the president of Oklahoma State University:

Dear Chris,
I noted in this morning's *O'Collegian* that you made the three-mile layout in 14:16.9 at the meet in Ames, to set a new record.

Congratulations and best wishes in future engagements. We are proud of your record at OSU!
Sincerely yours,
Robert B. Kamm
President

In 1966, Chris had achieved notoriety for both his dedication to the sport of running and his achievements in tough competition. He was working hard, improving his times and having fun. But, this wasn't the highlight for Chris in 1966. The best news was that he had discovered a new race—the 3000-metre steeplechase.

In the men's 3000-metre steeplechase competition, after beginning the race with a fraction of a lap, each runner runs seven complete laps. Each lap has four three-foot barriers and one water jump. Thus, over the 3000-metre race, the runner encounters 28 barriers that must be cleared and seven water jumps. Unlike a hurdle race, the barriers are fixed so if you stumble on a barrier, the barrier doesn't give way. The water pit is 3.66 m (12 feet) long and slopes upward from an initial depth of 700 millimetres (over 2 feet) to even with the track. Timing is everything.

The 3000-metre run is roughly equivalent to two miles so Chris was about to prove Coach Higgins correct. He would be one of the best two-milers to come out of Oklahoma. Chris had found his niche. Here was a race that combined Chris' running strengths—a distance runner with stamina.

Success in running the steeplechase didn't happen without hard work. OSU running colleague Ray Smith remembers Chris' dedication to running and the extra effort he put into it.

Chris pushed himself during his running workouts to achieve the most from his potential. He also had good foresight. The steeplechase race was not a normal event at the Big 8 Conference track meets in those days. However, after the track practices, Chris spent extra time running the hurdles.

Because it was a new running event, there was no steeplechase course at OSU and nowhere for Chris to practice so Coach Higgins improvised a course. He made some hurdles and put two posts and a beam on the infield to simulate the water jump. Throughout his training sessions, Chris could only imagine the sensation of landing in water.

April 9, 1966 was the first time Chris ran the 3000-metre steeple-chase in an official competition. The meet, the Arkansas Dual, was run at Stillwater. Chris took first place with a time of 9:00.2. His running partner Tom Von Ruden was second and brother Tip was third.

On April 22, 1966, the OSU track team was competing again at the Kansas Relays in Lawrence, Kansas. Chris was not on the relay team for this meet. Instead, he ran the 3000-metre steeplechase, finishing in third place at 9:23.4. The winner was Hylke Van der Wal, a runner from Manitoba, with a time of 9:09.5.

Chris ran the steeplechase again in Bloomington, Indiana on June 16, 1966, placing fourth in the 45th annual NCAA Track Championships. He was literally getting his feet wet in this event and loving it. On June 18, 1966, his success in running the steeplechase earned him further accolades. Chris was recognized and selected by a panel of American coaches for the All-American College Track and Field Team.

Jack Daniels, author of *Daniels' Running Formula*, lists four in-gredients that contribute largely to the success of a runner. They are: inherent ability—the genetic map inherited by the runner, the motivation to use that inherent ability, the opportunity to run, and good coach-ing—putting the runner in the right direction.

The steeplechase wasn't an easy race. Slogging through water and jumping barriers over a 3000-metre track had to be the most gruelling of runs. A runner in this race needed strength and endurance and good timing. Chris trained hard but the right genes helped. Zach Hilton McCubbins and his protégés appeared to have those tough stamina-ready genes in abundance.

McCubbins Heritage

THE MCCUBBINS FAMILY TREE STARTS WITH 6TH CENTURY 'ARCH DRUID' Cumin, the first in the McCubbins line of descent. I'll begin some centuries later with Zach—a great-great-grandfather of Chris.

Zach was born in 1826 in Tennessee but after his father died, he moved with his mother to Chicago. Zach was an entrepreneur. As a nineteen-year-old, he would head out to the prairies several times a year to round up cattle and sell them in Chicago. Once he saved enough money, Zach built a grocery store in a small community known as Yaleville in Jasper County, Illinois.

Zach served in the Civil War with an Illinois regiment of the Union Army. He was commissioned second lieutenant, then promoted to captain. He fought in the Wilderness Brigade and was wounded by a Spencer rifle. After the war, he returned to Yaleville, built a bigger store and married Mary Frances Clemmons. Looking for even more adventure, Zach and Mary moved to Arkansas to start a nursery business, but soon returned to Rogers, Arkansas as a grocer. In an early biographical reference of prominent Oklahomans, Zach is referred to as "a factor of wide influences in the community of Perry, OK, and has behind him a record of wisely conducted enterprises and rare devotion to the public good." Zach would have been proud of his great-great-grandson, Chris, who in addition to his exploits as a runner would continue to carry the torch of public good. Zach and Mary's son Churchill—the only boy in a family of four—carried the McCubbins name forward.

Churchill McCubbins, Chris' great-grandfather, made the Great Land Run of 1884 when Pawnee lands of five million acres were opened to settlement—the origin of the state of Oklahoma. To protect against claim jumpers, Churchill carried a shotgun. As Chris' mother Juanita described him,

> He was not about to let anyone jump his claim. He was a little man, but he was not, by any means, somebody to mess with. He was fast and he was somebody who could take care of himself.

He rode in on a horse and staked a claim about six miles north of Perry on Red Rock Creek. It was a good choice of land—high and dry. Soon afterwards, his dad Zach came from Arkansas and immediately set to building a store—a large two-storey structure—that sold groceries and Queen's Ware. Zach is buried in the Perry, Oklahoma cemetery.

Churchill married Lillie May Denman and moved into a home that Zach had built. Once land was claimed, the law was that someone had to be living on it or you lost the claim. Churchill and Lily raised a family of six. Clarence Raymond, Chris' grandfather, was the eldest of his six siblings.

It turned out that Clarence Raymond was also feisty and tough. He liked to fight. As a boy he would wander down to the black section of Perry and inevitably end up in a scrap. A boxing promoter saw his potential and began to groom Clarence as a prizefighter. To hide his fighting identity from his mother, Clarence fought under the name of 'Wild Cat Ferns.' He did very well as a boxer coming close to the title of world-welterweight champion. Clarence claimed the crown but a boxer in South America boasted that he was the sole champ. Clarence decided to settle the matter and meet this guy in the ring. According to Juanita,

> Clarence got on a ship in Seattle, Washington, and was on his way to South America. But, when he got down as far as San Francisco, all he had done was hang over the rail. He was just deathly sick. So, he got off in San Francisco and said the guy could have the title. He wasn't going on.

It was apparent that Clarence's fighting genes ran in the family. As Juanita explained, Dad Churchill really was someone you didn't want to mess with. One night, after a boxing match, Churchill decided to make his way to the dressing room to congratulate his son. At the door, Dad was confronted by two ex-boxer body guards.

"Where ya all goin, Pops," said one of them.
"Through that door to congratulate my son," said Churchill.
"No one gets in there," was the reply as they moved to block his entry.

That was the wrong thing to say. Churchill just punched them out and walked on in. It was said that he could hit a mule between the eyes and knock it out.

After his foray into boxing, "Wild Cat Ferns" was ready to settle down, find a wife and have a family and that's what he did. Clarence married Alma Muncy and they had two sons, Clarence Ferns and Robert Raymond.

Clarence Ferns was born in Red Rock, Oklahoma on December 19, 1916. His dad was operating the Pool Hall in Red Rock at the time of his birth. There were plenty of moves in the early years. The family lived for a short time in Superior, Arizona, where Clarence senior worked as a bit sharpener in a copper mine, and then to Perry, Oklahoma. When the opportunity arose and Clarence Ferns was six years of age, the family moved to Billings, Oklahoma where his Dad started in the produce and seeds business.

Clarence Ferns suffered an accident in Billings during his first summer there. An errant stone from a slingshot caught him in the eye. He was hospitalized and bedridden for some six weeks and ultimately lost sight in that eye. But the accident didn't slow him down. Clarence remembered the good times growing up in Billings, especially during the summer. He visited his grandparents in Kansas; he rode his own horse; he swam lots and he developed an early love of travelling the country—something he did every summer later in life with his own young family. As a youngster, he delivered papers for three years, saving enough money to buy both a bike and a violin. He rode the bike continuously but never did acquire the technique of playing the fiddle.

As a freshman in high school, Clarence played basketball and in his own words described how "he just missed being on the honor roll by a fraction. I had two C's which kept me off." The next year in high school, he was the class president, played both basketball and football and made the honor roll.

Clarence graduated from high school in the early thirties, at the height of the Great Depression. He worked in the family business and at any other jobs he could get, saving as much as he could. His dream upon graduation was to enter Oklahoma State University. When the time came, he had saved enough money for board and tuition but unforeseen circumstance wreaked havoc on that dream. The bank that was holding his savings declared bankruptcy. There was no recourse—no banking insurance in those days to recoup the loss. Clarence had to work harder, save harder and borrow. He attended university for three years, often eating only one meal per day to afford the luxury. He graduated in accounting with honours from Oklahoma State University. Prior to opening his own accounting practice in Enid, Oklahoma in 1947, Clarence worked as an accountant in both the public and private sector.

Clarence never forgot how people reached out to help him during his university years. Later, when he learned of a young person who was qualified to attend university but couldn't afford the tuition, Clarence provided the funds. He also devoted much of his leisure time to worthy causes such as Cub Scouts and the church.

The church was an important part of his life that provided Clarence with faith, hope and especially love—for this is where he met Juanita Snider. They courted for over a year and were married on June 4, 1939. Rilla was born on February 28, 1941, Tipton on July 9, 1944 and Philip Winston on October 10, 1958.

In Enid, Garfield County, Oklahoma, at 9:52 in the morning, at St. Mary's Hospital on November 22, of 1945, Juanita McCubbins' sister, Dr. Hope Ross, delivered Raymond Chris McCubbins. The official certificate of birth provided further details. Dad Clarence was 29 years of age and Mom was 27 at the time of his birth. Dad was still working for the Internal Revenue "Government" and Mom was listed as a "Hwf."—a housewife whose "industry or business" was listed as "own home". "Yes," a solution of silver nitrate was used in the eyes and "yes," a blood test for syphilis was made and the written order on the birth certificate "Do Not Give Result of Test" was followed. Older siblings Rilla and Tipton were anxious to meet their new brother.

Mom, Juanita Snider, was born April 3, 1918 in Vonore, Tennessee. Her father was Henry Tipton Snider.

Snider Family Heritage

HENRY TIPTON MARRIED IRIS ELLIS AND THEY HAD FIVE CHILDREN—
Hope, Raymond, Edwin, Juanita and Winston, who died at birth. The
family lived on a farm in Vonore, Tennessee.

Juanita's life was turned upside down when she was nine years old.
Her sister Hope left for college at Athens Tennessee and her mother
contracted pneumonia and died. Nathan, Juanita's cousin got typhoid
fever from drinking contaminated water. His mother, Juanita's Aunt
Jane, was looking after him but Jane contracted tuberculosis and died
the next spring. Then Martha also passed on. Juanita's mother and her
aunts—Martha and Jane—had all died within one year.

Juanita's cousin Nathan was only nine years of age when his mother
Jane died. Nathan's dad worked away so Nathan was going to be home
alone for much of the time. Juanita's brother Raymond was twelve when
their mother died. To keep Nathan company, Juanita's dad Tipton allowed Raymond to move to Vonore and stay with Nathan. Subsequently,
Raymond and Nathan became more like brothers than cousins.

That left Edwin and Juanita at home with Dad. Henry Tipton was
busy and on the road as the local postman, so Juanita assumed the task
of managing the household at an early age.

She and Edwin were close and Juanita had fond recollections of
her times growing up with her brother. As Juanita described, it is apparent that there were strong genes of strength and endurance from the
Snider clan.

Edwin was a good swimmer. He was Olympic calibre but he never
had the opportunity. By the time we were in junior high and high

school age, we had outgrown the swimming hole at the farm and had graduated to the sandbar on the [Little] Tennessee River, a mile down the Tellico from our house.

Now, a lot of the streams in Tennessee have either mud bottoms or rock bottoms; but this one had a big, sandy beach and a lot of shade. There was a huge tree that someone had climbed and put a rope on. And if you climbed up in the tree and got a hold on the rope, you could swing a way out over the river. Where it was deep enough, you could do any kind of a dive you were capable of doing.

Straight across the river from the big tree was Indian Head Rock [Wildcat Rock]. It was dark in color, and it had a point that stuck out on it that kind of looked like a nose. When you got up there to dive off, it was kind of like you see people in Acapulco doing. So, you had to swim the river, climb up through all the underbrush to get up on top of the rock.

Ed [Edwin] always needed to be challenged; and one day, when we were down at the sandbar, somebody said, "I'd give fifty cents for a good, cold drink of water."

Well, Ed heard him and says, "Do you mean that?"

"Sure, I'd pay fifty cents for a good, cold drink of water."

So Ed says, "Okay, give me a cup and I'll get you one."

The well was on the other side of the river and by the time you get across the river and down to the spring—it would probably be about two blocks. So, somebody got Ed a cup. He swam across the river and down to the spring. Well, that wasn't any great big deal because you were going down the stream on a pretty good current but he did have to manage to angle into the spring.

Coming back was another story. He had to get this cup of water, hold it up in one hand, swim upstream against a pretty good current, and not spill the water.

Well, everybody at the sandbar was watching him. There was no way he could dump the water and dip up new water out of the river. So he made it. He brought the guy back his cup of water, and the guy paid him fifty cents.

This Sunday swim got to be a regular thing—almost every Sunday afternoon. Everybody would go to the sandbar to see if Ed Snider could go and get a cup of water. Well, one afternoon he had gone and brought back three cups of water and he was beginning to look pretty tired and somebody was trying to get him to go back after the fourth cup. And I could tell he wasn't too crazy about it, but neither did he ever want to be a chicken.

Fortunately, somebody who knew Ed came up with a good excuse and talked him out of that last swim—a good thing since there could have been cramps and he would have gone down and there was nobody there who could have got him out. But Ed was always disappearing on us. That was a familiar cry at our house, "Where's Ed?" "Where's Ed?" I remember one particular day when this happened.

You always went to the river to look first for him. So somebody went down and there were his clothes on the bank of the Tellico River. So we knew he hadn't fallen in and drowned and it wasn't likely that he was gonna swim upstream in the Tellico. I don' know why Dad didn't get the skiff and go down the river to look for him but he didn't.

So Mother got on the highway which was just a two-lane blacktop road, and headed downstream. You couldn't walk along the riverbanks. There was just too much undergrowth and probably poison ivy and everything else. By the time Mother got down to the bridge over the Tellico, where it ran into the [Little] Tennessee, Ed had swum that mile all the way from our farm down to the Tennessee River.

Ed wasn't very old 'cause Mother died when I was nine and this was quite a while before Mother died. And so, by standing on the bridge Mother could see up the Tellico quite a little ways and watch for him. I expect by this time she was about scared to death and madder than an old wet hen 'cause she could get that way.

Well, when Ed got down to the bridge and got out, Mother was waiting for him. We were all in the yard watching for him. If you looked across the river bottom where our neighbour had a corn patch, you could see the highway more than a half a mile down there where it came out of the woods and Ed was trying to outrun her, but I think he was a little tired by this time and he was as naked as a chicken that's just been picked.

And mother had a switch. She was pretty good with a switch and every time Edwin had to slow down, he would get another switch. Well, he was barefoot and walking on hot tar and on the gravel and mother was right behind him. Now she could go a pretty good clip herself and by the time they got home, which was a mile from where he got out of the river, he looked kinda like a red-striped zebra.

One time, Ed's daredevil acts just about finished him off. The kids, when they were in high school, used to think it was great fun to jump on the train at the railroad crossing and ride it down to the depot and jump off again. It wasn't very far, maybe six or eight blocks, but on this particular day, it was raining and the train was going a little faster than it usually did. So Ed jumped on but his feet slid off and his legs went under the wheels of the train.

The thing that saved him was he had an old slicker raincoat on and it kept pushing his legs in front of the wheels until he could finally get them out. But while he was doing that his head was bumping on the cross ties and by the time he got to where he could turn loose of that train and get off, his head was a mess.

Doc McCollum had always been our doctor there in town and we found him and he had Ed set in the barber chair. The barber shaved Ed's head and Doc McCollum, in the barber shop, sewed it up.

Now he looked like a patchwork quilt. Dad and I sat there and watched them and Ed was not about to let out a yelp. He just gritted his teeth and let them sew and I don' know if they even deadened it or not.

Ed had a really thick head of hair and it all came back. I bet he had a lot of scars but you were never going to see them.

1967: Chris' Great Running Adventure

ON FRIDAY, JANUARY 13, 1967, THE *DAILY O'COLLEGIAN* ANNOUNCED THE 12 students at Oklahoma State University who were to be honoured through an outstanding achievement award. They had achieved recognition in some facet of university life and were selected by staff. Chris was one of the twelve. He was selected for "his outstanding acclaim as a harrier."

Here was further honour in addition to his 1966 designation as an All-American in steeplechase.

One month later, at the Missouri-OSU meet in Columbus, Chris ran the one-mile in 4:14.4 for a first place and followed that with a new meet and field house record in the two-mile with a time of 8:57.2.

The OSU *Daily O'Collegian* interviewed Chris for an article that appeared on February 23, 1967, "OSU Distance Ace Shows Improvement":

"The only reason I run is because I couldn't do anything else as a kid," is the modest answer Oklahoma State's lanky distance ace Chris McCubbins gives to queries about his start in track.

The OSU psychology major with B-plus grades stated that as a ninth-grader he went out for several sports, but never made the team. He was, in fact, the only little leaguer in town who didn't get a single hit in five years! He added that he must be over compensating now.

In high school, McCubbins' fastest mile was 4:24.2 and 2:05.6 was his best half- mile time. He finished 33rd in the state high school cross country meet. Chris attributes his sudden improvement to better conditioning and harder work.

"I run now because I love it," explains McCubbins. "When it quits being fun I'll quit."

The spring of 1967 was turning out to be a productive time in running. On March 4 he ran first in the two-mile at the Big Eight Indoor Track Meet in Kansas. His time was 9:02.2—a meet record. The past standard of 9:03.1 was set by OSU's Miles Eiserman in 1959. At the NCAA Indoors meet on March 10, the competition was tougher in the two-mile. Even though Chris had a time of 8:52.4, it was only good enough for fifth place. Gerry Lindgren of Washington State University set a winning time of 8:31.6. Then, Chris ran the one-mile race for OSU at the Triangular Meet with Rice, OSU and Lamar Tech in Houston, Texas. For a race that he appeared to be finished with, Chris attained first place with a time of 4:07.8.

On April 1, Chris ran the three-mile in the Big Eight Meet at Austin, Texas. His first place time was 13:38.7, over 25 seconds under the best time in meet history.

Then, on April 8, in Lawrence, Kansas, Chris returned to his niche event—the 3000-metre steeplechase—at the 43rd annual Kansas Relays. Coming in first, he set a new meet record of 8:46.6. The old record of 8:56.3 was set by Hylke Van der Wal in 1964. This appeared to be Chris' first competitive steeplechase race of 1967. He ran some 13 seconds ahead of second-place finisher John Mason of Fort Hays State College.

Chris dropped out of a 10,000-metre race at the same meet earlier in the week. He was evidently bothered by blisters but his main reason was the desire to be ready for the steeplechase run.

Chris was featured in an article in *The Enid Morning News* of Thursday, April 27, titled "One of the Best Runners in Big Eight Track, Chris McCubbins Thrives on Extra Work."

Chris McCubbins, Enid and Oklahoma State, and Glen Ogden of Missouri have become two of the best distance runners in Big Eight Track.

McCubbins ran 8:46.6 in the 3,000-metre steeplechase at the Kansas Relays, smashing the meet record by almost 10 seconds and establishing an all-time Big Eight best in the event. His time was only 4.6 seconds slower than the national intercollegiate record.

At the Texas Relays, he won the three-mile in a meet record 13:38.7, also an all-time best for the event in the Big Eight.

McCubbins is unusual in that he thrives on extra work. He runs faster when he competes in two events in one day. His best mile, 4:06.4, came on a day when he knew he'd be coming back later in the three-mile.

His favourite event is the steeplechase, and that's also unusual. The event isn't on the card at the Drake Relays, so he'll enter the three-mile, going for a triple crown, of sorts.

"Enid Senior Captains Track" was the title on a one-page OSU newsletter.

Chris McCubbins, senior distance runner at OS, has been named 1967 track captain of the Cowboys as the Pokes prepare for Big Eight championship action at Norman May 19-20.

Then from the *Oklahoman*—

McCubbins, who will be going in the three-mile at the Big Eight Championships in Norman, intends to bid for a place on the USA 1968 Olympic Games in Mexico City. Presumably he would be competing in the steeplechase.

At Norman, on May 4, Chris again ran the mile race—as well as the three-mile. He attained first place with respective times of 4:14.2 and 14:09.3. For the three-mile, Chris beat his old meet record set in 1966 of 14:30.8. In the one-mile, he tied with teammate Tom Laubert.

In the *Oklahoma Journal*, Friday May 5, journalist Phil Ford described how the one-mile ended in a dead heat.

Only an hour earlier McCubbins "tied" teammate Tom Laubert with a 4:14.2 mile. Holding a small lead and preserving plenty of energy for the finish, McCubbins waited for Laubert near the finish and the two Cowboys matched strides the last 20 yards for a dead heat.

There was an accompanying photo showing Chris with a major grin—a mischievous smile that implied "Hey, we're having some fun out here, so what's the fuss?" He had waited for his teammate to share in the glory of the race. It wouldn't be the only time that Chris would orchestrate such a race ending.

Chris received the Outstanding Trackman Award for 1967 at the OSU All-Sports Banquet in mid-May 1967 and shortly thereafter, on May 20, he ran the three-mile at the Big Eight Conference meet in Norman. He attained first place with a time of 13:51.9, knocking 12 seconds off his 1966 time. His time paled relative to his 13:38.7 record run of several weeks ago but was still his third best time.

> "I was just going for a win," he said. "That last lap came from my guts. I was tired at the finish."

After this race, Chris indicated that this might be his last three-mile race of the season. He planned instead to run the 3000-metre steeplechase in every meet he could find for the rest of the season. His goal was to win the NCAA championship in the steeplechase event.

In the spring of 1967, Chris, as a potential competitor in the 1968 Olympic Games, was invited to the US Army's high-altitude training camp in Alamosa, Colorado. Alamosa has about the same altitude, 7500 feet, and climate as Mexico City, where the Olympic Games were to be held in 1968.

Coach Jack Daniels from the University of Minnesota was leading the exercise. Daniels' dissertation research in 1968 focused on the testing of 26 of America's best distance runners. Fifteen of this group actually made it to the Olympics, so it is clear they were the fittest of the fit. One of the key metrics of fitness is referred to as VO2max. It's a measure of aerobic fitness. The average sedentary young adult male has a VO2max of about 44 millilitres of oxygen per kilogram of body weight per minute ($ml \cdot kg^{-1} \cdot min^{-1}$). The average value for the 26 runners at Alamosa was 78.6, far above that of the typical sedentary male. Chris' VO2max happened to be exactly equal to the mean of that group at 78.6. Some in that group had values above 80 and the lowest was 73.

It was expected that the typical adult will lose about one unit of that value each year beyond the age of 40, so at age 50, a 78.6 value should be down to about 53 ml/kg.

During the initial testing, there was an instance of Chris' stamina and perseverance in difficult conditions. Jack Daniels tells the story.

> One time when I was testing Chris in the lab, I mistakenly had the breathing apparatus set in reverse, so it was not possible to breathe in any air during a hard run on the treadmill. Chris said nothing, but after a minute of running [without being able to breathe], he finally stopped to ask if it always felt that bad to run that particular test. I can't imagine anyone lasting an entire minute, not breathing, while running pretty hard, and assuming that is how it was supposed to feel.

The high-altitude testing experiment wasn't all hard work and no play. One night, Jack and Chris attended a small-town dance where he remembered Chris being all over the floor. Not dancing all over the floor, but actually crawling and squirming all over the floor, not unlike an alligator or snake might respond to the music—and he wasn't intoxicated. Chris loved music and the interpretation of dance. Later in his career he would have the chance to pass on his creativity to a younger audience.

Chris was in good company with other top-class competitive runners—OSU teammate Tom Von Ruden, Kansas State's Conrad Nightingale, Oregon's sub-four-minute miler Wade Bell, Jim Ryun, record-breaking miler from the University of Kansas and Tom Heinonen of Minnesota.

Chris said that the altitude slowed him by a minute and 17 seconds on his best three-mile time. After his training, he improved his initial high-altitude time by 30 seconds.

While training at high altitude, Chris ran a marathon, the 26-mile endurance run. It's the first and possibly the last time he ran this race. He just didn't feel comfortable in this length of race and never changed his mind over all his years of running.

The Alamosa Olympic project training committee was also paying attention to the outcomes of the high-altitude training. They were a group trying to persuade national Olympic officials to train the track team in Alamosa for the 1968 games in Mexico City.

There was some question at the end of the day as to whether high-altitude training really helped a runner. There was a contention that the value of training at altitude was lost after several weeks back at sea level. In retrospect, Coach Jack Daniels, the expert on high-altitude training, made the following observation based on Chris' results.

> Chris completely showed that the value of training at altitude was not lost after a short period of time at sea level. During five weeks at altitude Chris improved his sea-level three-mile time by 14 seconds. However, instead of losing that improvement after some weeks back at sea level, Chris had his best-ever cross-country season, and then followed that by winning collegiate nationals in the steeplechase the next spring, and that summer was also Pan American Games champion in the steeplechase. So much for losing it after a few weeks back at sea level.

Chris returned from the high-altitude training and competed in the June 15 National College Athletics Association (NCAA) meet at Brigham Young Stadium in Provo, Utah. He set a new national record in the 3000-metre steeplechase with a first place time of 8:51.4. Running friend Conrad Nightingale placed second at 9:00.0.

There was another controversy brewing that night overshadowing the exploits of the track. Nine year-old Phil McCubbins, brother of Chris, was in the stands with his parents. He recalls the commotion on the field over Dick Fosbury's participation in the high jump. Fosbury had perfected the 'flop' as an alternative to the 'scissor' or 'western role' technique. Now, five years after perfecting the parabolic leap, there was still controversy over both its legality and safety. On the field, Fosbury was unaware of the controversy.

"I'm sure that there was a buzz going around. Even though we were jumping at the far end of the infield, away from the stands, as an athlete on the field, I was never aware at that time that some officials were having any such discussions at all. They did not approach me or ask me anything.

Virtually every meet since 1963, when I began evolving my technique in high school, had the officials pulling out the rulebook to check if this was legal. It was. And the landing pit environment was evolving from sawdust and wood chips toward foam chunks, to the 'Portapit' construction."

Next year, at the 1968 NCAA Championships, Fosbury did place first in the high jump and then went on to win gold at the '68 Olympics in Mexico.

"While my victory in '68 raised the awareness, and therefore the concern of safety, I was comfortable with jumping higher than 7 feet in sawdust. Yet everyone seemed to overlook the pole vaulters falling from 10 feet higher, also on their backs. It is sport and sometimes we take risks."

Back to the steeplechase, past champion Brigham Young runner, Bob Richards, hadn't fared well in the race.

A *Deseret News* article of Saturday, June, 1967 had the following take on Brigham Young's past steeplechase champion Bob Richards and Chris' strategy.

Bob Richards of BYU, the defending steeplechase champion, was another hardship case. He was leading the pack some 30 yards after about four-and-one-half laps when he caught a hurdle and suffered leg contusions and abrasions. He finished out of the money.

Steeplechase winner Chris McCubbins who won the event in a new record of 8:51.4, said he was amazed at Richard's fast start. "I was running a conservative race. I knew exactly what I was going to do at this altitude, because I had been running at 7,500 feet in

Alamosa, Colorado for nearly two weeks. I felt real good coming down to this altitude."

Shortly after this NCAA championship event, Chris was once again selected for the All-American College Track and Field Team in the 3000-metre steeplechase.

On June 23, 1967 in Bakersfield, California at the Amateur Athletic Union's track and field championships, Chris placed sixth in the 3000-metre steeplechase. Pat Traynor of the US Air Force won the race with a time of 8:42.0 and Conrad Nightingale was second at 8:43.8. Perhaps Chris was saving his strength for the Pan American Games trials in Minneapolis.

The Pan Am Trials for track and field were held at the University of Minnesota in Minneapolis on July 15 and 16. Chris ran the 3000-metre steeplechase in 8:39.6 at the Trials for a national collegiate record and a berth in the Pan American Games. Soon afterwards, Chris was on the plane for Winnipeg, Canada. He was with good company: long jumper Ralph Boston, 1500-metre speedster Tom Von Ruden, fellow steeple-chaser Conrad Nightingale, 800-metre runner Wade Bell, sprinter John Carlos, pole-vaulter Bob Seagren and 5-km and 10-km distance runner Van Nelson. Prince Philip, as the Queen's designate, was already in Winnipeg preparing to open the games on July 22.

There was also a new 15,000-seat stadium in place—built for the 5th Pan-Am Games complete with a synthetic 440-yard, eight-lane track. The resilient all-weather Tartan track—approved by the International Amateur Athletic Federation—was developed by the 3M Company. It was the first time that a synthetic track surface had been allowed in international competition. The facility also boasted of "Photosprint," the latest Omega technology for timing of events. The official program of the Games described this pre-digital innovation.

This device records on film the entire finish of each race, showing clearly the place and time of each competitor. In just 45 seconds after each race, the processed film is ready for enlarging and projecting, showing each athlete and his time to the hundredth of a second.

The athletes were billeted at Kapyong Barracks, the Canadian Army base located in south Winnipeg. Chris had trained hard throughout the week and decided to relax on the Saturday, July 29, the night before his race. He dropped in on the Village Cabaret where the athletes unwound. The party was in full swing and before long Chris was dancing the night away with a young attractive Pan Am volunteer, Marie Mackintosh. He walked Marie back to her home on Queenston Street and asked her if she wanted to see him run his race, the steeplechase, the next day at the University of Manitoba.

"I'll be there," she said, with little idea of what the race was or how this new friend might run.

Sure enough, Marie was in the stands on Sunday, ready for the race. Local Manitoban runner Grant Towns was also there, assessing the chances of competitors in the 3000-metre steeplechase. Of the two American runners, Chris McCubbins and Conrad Nightingale, Grant chose Nightingale over McCubbins.

"He appeared to be the smoother runner. I just went on appearance."

Chris ran away from Nightingale and won the gold medal with a first-place time of 8:38.2. It was both a Pan Am record and a Canadian record. Later, Towns would share living space with Chris and a number of other "Yellow Snow" runners. I wonder if he ever told Chris about his Pan Am pick—Nightingale over McCubbins.

Marie was also amazed at Chris' success. Typically, Chris hadn't talked about his running abilities, so the win and the gold medal were a complete surprise.

Nightingale of Kansas University fame and Chris were good friends by this time. In a press interview, Chris said that the two of them had a pact to tie the race. But at some point, Chris looked around to discover that Conrad had fallen back, so Chris decided not to wait for him. In an interview following the win, a journalist asked Chris about his reason for looking back but Chris didn't mention the pact. Instead he said,

> I'm most happy with my time, which is the best I have ever run. Yes, I started to look behind on the last lap, but only to see how Conrad

Nightingale was doing. There was no hope of my beating Gaston Roelants' world record today and I don't know if I can ever achieve this goal.

His 8:38.2 time at the Pan Am Games was getting closer to the winning time of 8:30.8 in the 1964 Olympics in Tokyo. The only better time for American steeplechasers during 1967 was by American Air Force runner Pat Traynor, who set a national record of 8:32.4.

There were only a few days to relax with Marie in Winnipeg after the Pan Am win: dining at Rae & Jerry's Steak House, strolling through Assiniboine Park and then flying to Montreal for the upcoming Europe vs. Americas Track and Field Meet. Tall, tanned and clean-cut in blue blazer, grey slacks and white shirt and tie, he looked the All-American youth as well as the All-American athlete that he was. It was an image with a short life. In later years, Chris became the most unlikely candidate for dress-up. Suits, ties and especially dress shoes made him cringe.

The Montreal meet was a first for a Europe-America competition and it appeared that the Europeans were ready whereas the Americans were not. It was held at the Autostade and was happening while the Montreal Expo 67 was in full swing. There was less than an enthusiastic turnout for the American team—21 athletes—about half the team. There was some controversy between the athletes and the AAU about air tickets and the process of reimbursement of funds. There were no new uniforms. Patches, identifying the team as Americas, had been sewn over the Pan Am and USA insignias. Even fan interest was low. There were some 8000 people in a facility that held 25,000.

Many of the athletes were tired from a gruelling agenda leading up to this race. There were the Commonwealth Games in Los Angeles, the AAU championships in California, the Pan Am Trials in Minneapolis and the Pan Am Games in Winnipeg. Then, after the Europe vs. Americas in Montreal, there was a series of European meets planned for the United Kingdom, Germany and Italy.

On August 9, the day prior to the Montreal meet, Chris got a telegram from Winnipeg.

Good luck I know you'll win. Thinking of you. Write. I have cut out all your newspaper clippings and will send them later. Hope you are having a marvellous time and have seen Expo. Marie

As it happened, the athletes didn't see much of Expo 67. As John Underwood wrote in an August 21 article in *Sports Illustrated* titled "Pop Fare for a Popular Fair."

There was no provision, either, for any kind of hospitality, or even a tour of Expo. It would cost too much, said one Expo official and, besides, they would not have time to make such a tour. It would take five hours, he said. Instead the athletes were given passes and left to run the maze alone. Sprinter Jerry Bright said a bunch of the guys went to the La Ronde entertainment center at Expo for a couple of hours on Monday night and that was that.

Overall the Americas team lost the competition to Europe but there was one bright light. Chris was able to overcome the controversies and win the gold medal in the 3000-metre steeplechase. His first place time of 8:44.1 gave him a berth on the US team for the upcoming European games. He was one of four steeplechasers on the squad. The others were Pat Traynor, Conrad Nightingale and Bob Price.

The gold medal win in Montreal was an important running accomplishment for Chris. It was a more significant win because of the participants. In an interview prior to his 1999 induction into the Manitoba Sports Hall of Fame, Chris cited the above race in Montreal as a pinnacle, one surpassing the Pan Am Games win because it came against tougher competition. It was an opportunity to make an impact on the world scene.

At the European Games, races were planned in a number of European track centres. Due to an injury suffered in the first race, Chris ran only in Dusseldorf, Germany. He had been bumped by a German competitor while leaping a hurdle and ended up face first in the water. Then he fell in a second water jump. Although he and Nightingale had been leading the race up to this point, recovering from the fall cost him valuable time. Chris finished at 8:54, well off his record Canadian times. Later in the European Games at a meet in Viareggio, Italy, Chris' team-mate Conrad Nightingale clocked a career low race-winning time of 8:40 in the 3000-metre steeplechase.

Conrad and Chris became close friends after a year of running together. After the European Games, Conrad visited Enid and enjoyed a steak dinner with Chris and his parents. In the Sports Talk column of *The Enid Morning News*, (August 27, 1967) Nightingale is quoted as saying

> It was getting pretty tiring. You'd get up in the morning, look across the room and know you were going to have to try and outrun that guy again.

Although he was out of action for the rest of 1967 as a result of the Dusseldorf accident, Chris still had one of the best running years of his life. He was only 21 years old. The US Olympic trials were looming and he was surely a candidate for the American steeplechase team. He also had to finish his final year of Arts at OSU.

September '67—Back to OSU

CHRIS RETURNED TO OSU FOR A FINAL YEAR OF STUDIES. THIS WAS HIS fifth year at the university but he was ineligible for the OSU track team. He was still a prime candidate for the 1968 Olympic Games. His steeplechase time at the Pan Am Games in Winnipeg placed him in an elite category of runners.

Chris was in touch with his long-time friend and running partner Ray Smith, who was also back for his final year of Engineering at OSU. Chris wondered if Ray wanted to share accommodation for their final year of studies. Ray said yes and went looking. He discovered that one of the athletic trainers, Doc Johnson, had a garage apartment for let for the school year. The apartment was small, as it had been built originally for a single vehicle, perhaps in the early 1940s. Nevertheless, it had three compact rooms—a kitchen, bathroom and bedroom.

The kitchen had a stove, sink and a small table with two chairs. This was a time prior to fast-food dining so Chris and Ray would have to do their own cooking. The bathroom had a tub but no shower and there were two single beds squeezed into the bedroom. They took it.

During the Christmas break of 1967, Chris travelled back from Enid to Winnipeg to stay with Marie and her family. Although the visit was short, he didn't miss an opportunity to compete. On December 30, he ran the two-mile at the Saskatchewan Centennial Indoor Games in Saskatoon. He placed second with a time of 9:02.4 after a tough battle with Australian runner George Scott. This is how the *Winnipeg Free Press* on Monday January 1, 1968 described the race.

George Scott of Australia turned on a strong kick Saturday with half a lap remaining and scored a 10-yard victory over Chris McCubbins of OSU. The spurt came after two dozen laps during which the two men ran almost shoulder to shoulder, trading small leads several times. The tactic wore down the others in the field of five.

Scott said afterwards that he had no race plan except "to watch McCubbins. Chris always tries something different. Tonight he was changing his pace figuring it might kill me. It almost did."

Chris didn't do a lot of competitive running in the early months of 1968. He was undoubtedly spending more time on his academic studies to ensure graduation in the spring. Then he would start serious training for the USA Olympic trials.

Chris ran in the John Jacobs Invitational meet at Norman, Oklahoma in mid-April, of 1968. He ran the 3000-metre steeplechase in 9:12.3 for second place. His running buddy Conrad Nightingale placed first at 9:07.1. Both runners were off their best times. Prior to the race, in an interview with *The Sunday Oklahoman* (April 13, 1968), Nightingale predicted that Chris would "beat me by a minute."

Later in the month at the 43rd Kansas Relays, Chris and Conrad, both prime candidates for the US Olympic team, ran again in the open 3000-metre steeplechase. Chris was just coming off a period of injury. The order was the same as the last race. Conrad was first with a time of 8:52.8 and Chris second at 8:59.8. The day previous, Chris ran in the 10-km race, placing fifth with a time of 31.36.8. Jim Murphy was first at 29:51.6. The *Kansas City Times* of April 19, 1968 described the race. Chris is quoted about his fifth-place showing.

"I was bothered by side cramps and I had to stop and walk a couple of times. I didn't want to force myself because I want to be ready for the steeplechase." Chris has been battling some physical problems of late. He tore a groin muscle. Then he found he had a slipped vertebra in his neck. When he finally overcame these problems, a bout with the flu forced him to start his training program a week late. "This was only my second race since January when I ran in Boston.

I ran the two-mile in 9:06.2 and finished dead last. I trained hard last week and I feel like I'm really in good shape. I think I'm ready.

I would like to make the Olympics, but that's just a dream. There are so many good guys that it would depend on a lot of things for me to make it."

Interestingly, there is a photo from the Boston meet of broad jumper Ralph Boston. On the side of the photo Chris has written:

Ralph cheered me on and encouraged me to win! He kind of inspired me! He also won the Pan-Am broad jump. Go U.S.A.!

Later that spring, Chris placed first in the two-mile race at the Inaugural North-East Boosters Club meet in Monroe, Louisiana. His time was 8:52.8 after a close race with Olympian Oscar Moore who ran at 8:53.1.

On May 26, 1968 at OSU Stillwater, Chris is listed in the commencement ceremonies program as receiving his Bachelor of Science in Psychology. Shortly after, Chris and Marie left for Lake Tahoe—the training site for the 1968 Olympic Games. Chris would be preparing for competition in the 3000-metre steeplechase at the Olympic trials. Of course, he didn't wait to get there to ensure that he was maintaining his fitness. After setting up the tent, in some fairly remote sites, Chris would leave Marie to go for a run. His mind was focused on the upcoming Olympic trials and hers on the potential of wild animals visiting the campsite.

The American Athletic Union (AAU) listed the qualifying times and positions to gain entry to the trials in the 3000-metre steeplechase—Chris was ranked fifth at 8:39.8.

On June 29, at the South Lake Tahoe Coliseum, Chris placed eighth in the US Olympic track and field trials with a time of 9:37.4. His dream of making the '68 US Olympic Team was over. George Young of Casa Grande won at 8:57.9.

High altitude running took its toll on times. Winner Young had set a previous Coliseum record on June 7, 1968 of 8:36.2.

Leading the field in the latter part of the race, Chris fell into a barrier. He dislocated his neck vertebrae and fractured a small bone in his leg. Amazingly, he finished, but undoubtedly under duress. This was the first incident where an untimely injury forced Chris out of the top placements in the race but didn't stop him from finishing. It would happen again. He was one tough competitor. That summer Chris returned to Winnipeg. It was time to rest and recuperate from injuries. The interval of calm was short-lived. Americans were fighting a war in Vietnam and young people like Chris were being called for duty.

Great-great-grandfather Zach McCubbins, 1826–1902. *Photo courtesy of the McCubbins family.*

Great-grandparents, Churchill (1860–1919) and Lillie McCubbins (1862–1946). Churchill made the Oklahoma land run. *Photo courtesy of the McCubbins family.*

Grandfather, Clarence Raymond McCubbins (1885-1961) also known in the world of welterweight boxing as 'Kid' or 'Wild Cat Ferns.' He was close to claiming the world welterweight championship. *Photo courtesy of the McCubbins family.*

Father, Clarence Ferns McCubbins (1916-2001). *Photo courtesy of the McCubbins family.*

At Cubs, Chris in an unofficial cool shirt, with his mother as leader and brother Tip, the tallest Cub behind. On the far left is Doug Greer. I wasn't able to identify the other two Cubs. *Photo courtesy of the McCubbins family.*

An Enid Jefferson School photo of nine-year old Chris from the 1954-55 school year. *Photo courtesy of the McCubbins family.*

Chris in the eleventh grade starting out as a runner. *Photo courtesy of the McCubbins family.*

A 1961–62 photo of Chris and his siblings. From the left: Tipton, Rilla, Phillip and Chris. *Photo courtesy of the McCubbins family.*

The Oklahoma State University cross country team at the 27th NCAA National Collegiate Cross Country Championships at Lawrence, Kansas, the site of Kansas University, November 22, 1965. Chris turned 20 years of age that day. He placed 5th in a field of 152 runners and was named to the All American Cross Country Team. From the left: Larry Farmer, Ray Smith, Tom Von Ruden, Coach Ralph Higgins, Chris, Tip McCubbins, Glenn Blakley. *Photo courtesy of the NCAA/T3 Media.*

The OSU Cross Country Team in action at the OSU Cross Country Jamboree Race at Hillcrest, Oklahoma on October 9, 1965. Chris ran the 4-mile course in 20:31, the best time for OSU runners. From left to right: Tom Von Ruden (OSU), Don Lakin (2nd at 19:40 from Fort Hays College), Chris, unknown USAF competitor, Glenn Blakley (OSU). *Photo courtesy of Sue Jacobsen.*

1965 Cross Country run showing some members of the Oklahoma State University team. From the left: Tom Von Ruden, Chris, Larry Farmer, Glenn Blakley, Danny Metcalf and Jim Metcalf. *Photo courtesy of Sue Jacobsen.*

Chris, at the high altitude training camp in Alamosa, Colorado, early 1967. He was one of twenty-six of America's best distance runners being tested for fitness by Dr. Jack Daniels. *Photo courtesy of photographer Richard M. Thomas.*

Chris, arriving for a 1st place finish in the 2-mile race at a Kansas Big Eight Indoor Track Meet, March 4, 1967. *Photo courtesy of Sue Jacobsen.*

The cover photo with Chris in the 3000-metre steeplechase at the 46th annual NCAA Track & Field Championships, June 1967 at the Brigham Young University Stadium—a first place finish and a new national record at 8:51.4. *Photo courtesy of the NCAA/T3 Media.*

Chris with friend and fellow-steeplechaser, Conrad Nightingale. *Photo courtesy of Sue Jacobsen.*

Called for Duty

ON A FRIDAY EVENING IN NOVEMBER, 1968, CHRIS RECEIVED A TELE-phone call from his mother advising him that his draft papers had been issued. He needed to report to the military board in Oklahoma. In Enid, Juanita had spoken to a woman employed by the board who explained that Chris' military induction notice had been sent to Alamosa, Colorado, his last known address. Chris had been in Lake Tahoe at the US Olympic trials during the spring of that year and now was back living with Marie at her parents' home in Winnipeg. Chris had until Monday—three days hence—to report to the military headquarters in Tulsa, Oklahoma.

It wasn't unusual to hear of Americans dodging the draft and re-locating in Canada. For some eligible draftees, the prospect of serving in the Vietnam War prompted the northern move to a safer haven. Chris wouldn't be part of this movement. He was going back home to honour his commitment. There was no other course of action in his mind. He was an American and this was his duty.

Due to the urgency of getting back to Oklahoma, Chris decided to catch a direct flight from Grand Forks. This meant hitchhiking along Highway 75 from Winnipeg to Grand Forks through blowing snow and cold winds. He was dressed in his green parka and toque and heavy mitts but you had to be impressed with not only his gutsiness for venturing out in this weather but also with his decision to honour his obligation to military service. There wasn't a heartbeat of hesitation. If he didn't go back, he was letting down a lot of people. Undoubtedly his patriot-ism played a big part, but he spoke most about the importance of the expectations of his parents—especially of his mother. Juanita was a role model who he never wished to disappoint.

Evidently, his mother was surprised by how quickly Chris returned home. She had been in further contact with the authorities.

> He was in Canada when his draft came up. He turns up with everyone else and the lady at the board [draft board] was going to postpone it—and they were surprised to see him—she had said "we'll get him next time"—but here he turns up—that's what it's like in a small town like Enid.

Chris arrived at the draft board office and there were three other young people meeting the call. That day there were two positions available for the Marines and one for the Army. Chris drew the Army card. He would soon be off for basic training.

Juanita recalled an experience some thirty years prior when her cousin Nathan volunteered for military service.

> I wonder if Chris remembered the story of my cousin Nathan. He graduated from Louisiana State University and was called up for the Second World War. He didn't want to go with the infantry so decided to try for a commission in the navy. He went to the recruitment office in Knoxville and met all of the requirements except one. Nathan didn't have a birth certificate. The recruiter said no problem, "I'll call my contact in Nashville and have him fetch the birth certificate."
>
> A short time later, the contact calls back. There is no record of birth for Nathan Hale Snider, born in Vonore on that date. The only one we have is a Joe Jackson Snider born on that date.
>
> Nathan couldn't figure out the root of the problem but told the recruiter that he would return to Vonore and look up old Dr. McCollum—the doctor who delivered him. He found Dr. McCollum and explained his dilemma and sure enough the doctor had an answer.
>
> "When you were born, your parents didn't come up with a name. I hounded them for one. 'Have you named the baby, yet?'"
>
> The answer was always the same. 'No, not yet.'"

"I was running out of time: I needed to get something in to the Bureau of Vital Statistics in Nashville. I guessed that the new baby would be named after both grand-pappies—Joe Jackson."

Mystery solved. But it does seem unusual that anybody can go all the way through college and be as bright as Nathan, and not even know his own name.

Chris entered the army on December 1, 1968 and became "SP4 McCubbins, Raymond C 442-46-4717." Life in boot camp must have been a shock, as the following letter home attests. It was a letter written on the back of an army photo.

Win, Mom, Dad
You might give one of these [photos] to Grandmother. I've already sent one to Marie. The holder for the big picture wouldn't fit. In our first physical fitness test, I ran my mile in combat boots in 4:46. We started going to the rifle range also last week. They have let up a lot on the harassment. But I haven't got much sleep as we have a bad barrack for cleaning up and skrewed [sic] up people in charge who get you up at 2:30 to get a job done by 9:30 that we finish about 7:00. Really bums me off. Not much else exciting happening. All of the pictures and another large one cost $13 which isn't too bad I guess.
—Chris

Chris completed his basic training at Fort Polk, Louisiana in February of 1969. During the training time, he learned of a military team of elite athletes who competed in a branch of the United States Army. These pentathletes run cross country, swim, ride, pistol shoot and fence. In retrospect, he had to be happy that he drew the Army card at induction. It gave him an option other than Vietnam.

Modern Pentathlon

CHRIS CONTACTED HIS FORMER COACH AND MENTOR JACK DANIELS TO glean more about the military's Modern Pentathlon Team and his chances of serving in this unit of the army. Daniels was a former US Olympian in the sport and felt that Chris had the necessary attributes to compete. According to coach Daniels,

> Chris was a good swimmer as well as being very talented as a runner, and during the Viet Nam conflict, when many American youngsters were being drafted into the service, Chris volunteered and as a former US Olympian in the sport, I was in a position to get him to spend a good deal of his Army time training for modern pentathlon.

The modern pentathlon has been an Olympic event since 1912. The event is staged over a five-day period during which there is competition in one sport per day. The two strength and endurance sports—swimming and running—are held on the last two days.

Legend has it that the sporting event has war-fighting origins. As Napoleon was leading his army on forays of conquer across Europe in the early decades of the 19th century, couriers on horseback were assigned to get mail and messages through the enemy lines. In the course of their duties, there was a host of encumbrances to foil the courier's task. Over long distances, horses that were either injured or just exhausted had to be replaced. Some even died in combat. Thus, the courier had to be a rider capable of handling strange and sometimes unpredictable animals. If a horse wasn't available, the courier continued the journey on foot—cross-country running over land and swimming across lakes and rivers.

If the enemy were encountered, the courier would have to fight his way through. He carried both a pistol and a sword for that purpose and had to be skilled in the use of both his revolver and his épée.

The modern pentathlon mirrors the travails of the earlier courier. For one athlete to have such a range of attributes and skills is unusual and takes a special breed of person. There is a need: for patience and shrewdness to shepherd a strange horse over a 1000-metre equestrian course, for stamina to run the 4000 metres over a challenging cross-country terrain, for strength to swim 300 metres, for accuracy and a calm and steady hand in the marksmanship of the pistol, and the quickness of a cat to win at fencing.

Chris completed his basic training at Fort Polk, Louisiana in February, 1969. He competed in the 1969 Council of International Military Sports (CISM) track and field championships in Ireland and Scotland in mid March of 1969. Upon his return from Europe, Chris was accepted into the military's United States Modern Pentathlon Team and was based at the US Modern Pentathlon Training Center at Fort Sam Houston, Texas.

In mid May of 1969, the families of Marie and Chris gathered in San Antonio Texas to witness and celebrate their wedding. There was good fellowship and a memorable boat ride on the Alamo River complete with an on-board Dixieland Band. The music might have been a bit loud for Chris that night. His fellow pentathletes had raised their glasses the night before at a traditional stag party and then had one last round at the Rabbit Habit, a local pub. Chris and Marie were married on May 17, 1969 at a ceremony in the Post Chapel at Fort Sam Houston, San Antonio Texas. Army Chaplain Paul officiated and Tipton F. McCubbins and Rilla M. Chaney acted as witnesses. On the way to a celebratory supper, the Texas winds began to blow, bending trees and blowing out neon signs. The Canadians thought it was the end of the world but locals knew it would soon be over, and sure enough, all was calm and the celebration proceeded.

Chris and Marie moved into an apartment outside of Fort Sam Houston at the US Modern Pentathlon Training Center. The Brooke Army Medical Center was and is part of the US Army Medical Command at Fort Sam Houston. As such, the base was a busy place. Choppers were landing continuously, bringing in the Vietnam-injured troops, especially those that required care at the Burn Center.

Chris commuted daily for pentathlon training in the morning and assigned military duties in the afternoon. Each athlete worked three to five days per week on regular assigned army duties. Chris had the task of managing gym activities—especially basketball—for the core soldiers assigned to the barracks as well as those who had recovered sufficiently from injuries to begin physical activities. Nevertheless, his main job was to perform as a pentathlete.

As Marie reflects, even though each of the athletes was elite in their chosen field, they had to adjust to competition in an array of events.

Chris had never fenced or ridden or shot but he had an advantage because of his running abilities. There was only one guy who was a world-class épée fencer—but he had never ridden a horse.

The equestrian competitions were tough on people like Chris who weren't riders. The horses were all donated and some were good but others were almost impossible to ride. I remember this one horse—St. Louis—who was so loveable but very difficult to ride. In competitions, you drew the horse that morning. There was a competition in Dallas and Chris drew St. Louis. Chris thought that it was all over because this horse would often throw the rider. What a surprise when he did a series of perfect jumps.

But Chris worked hard at training and over time improved enormously. He became a very good shot.

We had a lot of fun. I remember one night when one of the coaches came over to a party at our house and brought a bottle of champagne. He shot the top off and it went all over the carpet and all over me. That was just before Chris' parents visited. The carpet was really stained and we didn't want to be charged for damages. Juanita came up with the idea of soda to get it out of the carpet and thank goodness it worked.

The community of pentathletes were fun to be with but there was great paranoia because of the stakes—do well in competition or go to Vietnam.

Chris ran in a number of 5-km races and qualified for a trip to France and Ireland in this event. The Irish meet was held in Cork on July 8, 1969. Chris ran a great race at the Cork City Sports Meet and placed first with a 13:55.4 time. Second place went to T. O'Riordan, who ran at 14:9.5. This was a personal best for Chris in the 5-km. An Irish sports journalist reported that "this was a serious assault on the CISM championships to be held in France, July 12-13, 1969."

On July 19, 1969, at the Sheppard Inter-Service Track & Field Championships in Wichita Falls, Texas, Chris ran in the 3000-metre steeplechase. He placed first and set a new meet record of 8:59.1.

It took some time for Chris to become competitive in the swimming, shooting, fencing and horseback riding but Chris was an all-round good athlete and once he allocated training time for these events, results were good. Typically, Chris wasn't afraid of hard work and it paid off.

The *Enid Morning News* of Sunday, March 8, 1970 ran an article titled "Former OSU Steeplechase Champ Concentrates on Pentathlon." An inter-squad competition was held in January, 1970 at the Houston base and Chris finished fourth of nine competitors. This performance put him in contention for one of the top ten spots in the July 1970 nationals. Here is an excerpt from the press article.

> Howard Johnston, running coach for the modern pentathlon training center, explained Chris' potential in the following way:
>
> "Chris picked up over 1,400 points in the run this last intra-squad, nearly 200 points better than the next best pentathlete. That certainly helps his point total, but he couldn't have been up that high without four other pretty good sports.
>
> Chris had an ulcer which laid him up for three months late in '69, plus he hasn't been running that much even after he came back from Christmas holidays because he's been concentrating on his other four sports...but still he's most likely the best pentathlon runner in the world right now, or at least right up there with the best."

Quoted from the same *Enid Morning News* article, Chris provided some further insights regarding his physical condition and plans.

McCubbins said he's not really in good shape for running right now because he's swimming seven times a week, about 2,500 yards a workout, and only getting to run two or three times a week at the most.

"But right now I'm a pentathlete and doing what I need for that sport," he said.

He still hasn't decided on whether he'll concentrate on track or the pentathlon when he leaves the Army in September.

"How I do in the pentathlon this summer may decide for me," he says. "I hope to get my masters in psychology at the University of Manitoba and I kind of doubt whether they have pentathlon training facilities up there, so I think I will go back to some serious running for a few years and try the pentathlon on the side. A lot of pentathletes peak in their early 30s, so I still have some time to decide.

The same thing that will probably keep me from training in pentathlon in Canada—the lack of facilities—is what makes America's program in pentathlon weak in comparison to the European countries. The only place to train here is at Fort Sam Houston, and that means we can't really get a broad-based age group program going over the entire United States."

It was little wonder that Chris was sidelined with an ulcer. There was huge pressure on all the athletes to perform. Swimming was one of his weakest and most stressful areas. Chris' neck was sore from the turning to one side and that pain permeated his body and undoubtedly affected his performance in other events. The only redeeming fact was that all the athletes faced the same conditions.

The following table provides results for a mid-April meet in 1970 at Foxcatcher Farms.

DATE	LOCATION	MEET	EVENT	TIME	POINTS	PLACE	OVERALL
April 17-18/1970	Foxcatcher Farms, Media, Penn.	4th Triathlon Invitational & National Championships	Swim Shoot Run	2:46 10:48	872 180/800 1621	27/51 12/51 1/51	1st with 3293 points

The meet was hosted by John Du Pont the 31 year-old heir of the family's estate and participant in the pentathlon. Dr. Du Pont, former Marine and authority on birds, was also an ardent supporter of Olympic swimmers, wrestlers, modern pentathletes and triathletes. He was a competent athlete who loved the rigour of the sport and was convinced that American athletes could do better at world-class events. Du Pont had played host at Foxcatcher Farms to the 1967 National Modern Pentathlon Championships in addition to participating in those games. He finished 14th in the competition. It is alleged that pentathlon officials—undoubtedly out of earshot of Du Pont—referred to him as a competent dilettante.

Chris and the Army team stayed in New York City and he and others attended the Broadway musical *Hair*—much to the chagrin of Marie. Wives and significant others were not included on these competitive junkets.

Chris was featured in a news piece in the *Enid Daily Eagle* of April 21, 1970.

> McCubbins also placed second in a triathlon at West Point recently. Upcoming events for him include the Fourth Army meet at Lawton on May3 (he will run the steeplechase and either the three or six-mile run) and the Council International Sports Military (CISM) pentathlon trials at Fort Sam Houston, San Antonio, Texas, the last week of May.

In July of 1970, after three events, Chris scored as follows.

DATE	LOCATION	MEET	EVENT	TIME	POINTS	PLACE	OVERALL
July 13/1970	Fort Sam Houston Texas	Modern Pentathlon National Championships	Ride Fence Shoot		1000 875 868	5th place of 23 competitors	2743 points

Here are the results for the Lawton event of May 3, 1970. Chris placed second overall.

DATE	LOCATION	MEET	EVENT	TIME	POINTS	PLACE	OVERALL
May 3, 1970	Lawton Oklahoma	Fort Sill	Swim	2:42	904	11/36	2nd with
			Shoot		980	3/35	3148
			Run	13:02	1264	1/35	points

Jack Daniels was correct in supporting and promoting Chris as an athlete in the modern pentathlon. Chris was a serious competitor. As Daniels said,

> He didn't quite make it to the World Championships in that sport, but he was certainly close, and of course, always walked off with the running event of the five pentathlon events.

On September 2, 1970, Chris received a letter from the Department of the Army, Headquarters, Fort Sam Houston, Texas.

> The following individual is RELIEVED FROM ACTIVE DUTY not by reason of physical disability and transferred to the United States Army Reserve as indicated.

Chris was assigned to US Army Control Group (Annual Training) US Army Administration Centre, St. Louis, MO. His UMTS obligation was stated as six years. Given that he had served close to two years, this meant that his reserve obligation expired on December 1, 1974.

It appeared that Chris had applied for discharge so that he could return to college, but he agreed to serve on standby in the Army Reserves for another four years.

Chris and Marie arrived back in Canada through Emerson, Manitoba on September 10, 1970. It was time to get back to civilian living, plan for future studies and return to the fun of the run.

Back on Track

CHRIS WAS FREE OF THE GRIND AND DISCIPLINE OF LIFE IN THE MIL-
itary. He grew his hair long and tried to grow a beard—a life-long challenge. He settled for the long hair.

Chris was keen to keep involved in running—especially cross country. Running and his dedication to training was ingrained in his psyche.

He knew of Jim Daly, the executive director of the Winnipeg Pan
Am Games in 1967, and had learned of Daly's role as coach of the university cross country team. For Chris, running was still a major priority
so a meeting with Jim was at the top of the list. Daly recalled the occasion—the beginning of a long-lasting friendship.

I was in my office at the University of Manitoba and my secretary called.

"There's a Chris McCubbins here that would like to speak with you."

I figured it must be the runner Chris McCubbins. I had missed
the steeplechase race but was familiar with the name. As it turned
out it was the person who won the gold medal in 1967. Chris had
just finished two years in the forces doing the modern pentathlon
and wanted to get involved with the cross country-running team
at the U of M. So one of his questions was, "Where do you train?"

On Wellington Crescent, I replied—because most of the time we
are running on grass. And, like horses, it's better to be running on
grass. It's a lot easier on the body.

Chris beamed. "I love running on grass."

It turned out that Ralph Higgins, Chris' coach from OSU, had
a novel way of keeping his runners involved and motivated to run.
When the track team came out to practise, Chris would lead some

training runs. Higgins did some intervals and other set procedures, but mostly he wanted runners to run. So Chris would lead a run over hill and vale—but mostly on grass. When they returned, Higgins knew by their physical appearance—mostly the sweat—that they had had a good workout. Training on grass was a bonus for Chris.

When I knew Chris would be coming out, I invited Sheldon Reynolds. Sheldon knew of Chris and his running reputation and was just in awe. After about a half hour out on the course, I moved back to where Chris and several other runners were standing and there was Sheldon lying on the grass. He was spread out like an eagle—his rib cage was moving in and out like an accordion—his face was red and he just looked spent. When he saw me, Sheldon said, "What a workout!"

Without skipping a beat Chris replied, "What workout? That's just the warm-up."

Runner Karl Sproll remembered training indoors in the winter with the University of Manitoba track team.

We used to meet at the Gritty Grotto, the track in the basement of the Frank Kennedy Centre at the University of Manitoba. The track got its name from the dirt piled up on the sides. We spent a lot of time down there. I'll always remember the first time I came out to run. Chris had put up a hand-drawn sign titled GADRAD (Give a Distance Runner a Drink). You put your name on the side and then you would put in your daily distance run on the chart. Each runner was expected to do two miles per day. If you didn't make your quota the rule was that you threw 25 cents into the kitty for drinks for the guy with the most miles for the month. Chris was more of a mentor than a coach, and a great leader. He set out a program of training for each of the runners based in large part on the philosophy of his former coach Jack Daniels.

Chris had enjoyed his undergraduate years at Oklahoma State University where he majored in Psychology. His plan was to continue studies in

Psychology, and so he enrolled in the Arts faculty at the University of Manitoba to pursue post-graduate studies. In the fall of 1970, he registered in the master's program.

Chris was back running cross country but hadn't given up on the steeplechase. The 1972 Olympics were looming.

In late August, 1971, he competed in the 3000-metre steeplechase at the Canadian Senior & Junior Track & Field Championships, University of Manitoba Stadium. He placed first with a time of 8:49.0, not far off his 8:38.2 winning time in 1967.

Then in June, 1972, Chris placed sixth in the first heat of an Amateur Athletic Union meet in Seattle with a time of 8:40.8. It must have been a close and competitive race, since his former running pal Conrad Nightingale, then with the United States Air Force, placed second at 8:38.2. Chris had injured his Achilles tendon and was out of the competition for the 1972 Olympic Games. Olympic aspirations were dashed once more.

He never had a lot of patience sitting out an injury, always anxious to get back on the track as soon as possible. In retrospect, he probably should have waited but on July 22, in Toronto, he was entered in the Senior Canadian Championships also known as the Canadian Open Olympic Trials in 1972. Being an American citizen, Chris was welcome to compete at this meet but was ineligible for placement on the Canadian team. Chris ran in the 3000-metre steeplechase and won the only Manitoban gold. He had to recover from a fall to do it. With five laps to go that same left ankle buckled as he completed a hurdle and collapsed on to the grass off the track. Picking himself up, he chased the leaders. With some courage, he shook off his injury for the remainder of the race and proceeded to overtake the field, winning the only gold medal for Manitoba by 20 metres.

Unfortunately, the Achilles injury was serious. For the fall of 1972, Chris was on the sidelines awaiting surgery. He and Frodo had earned a rest.

Anyone who knew Chris in his early years in Winnipeg also knew his dog, Frodo. She was Texas born but spent most of her life in Winnipeg. She ran wherever and whenever Chris ran—summer at +28 degrees C and winter at -28 degrees C. Frodo was supposed to be a large hunting dog—a shorthaired silver-grey coated pure-bred Weimaraner—but that wasn't to be. She had the sleek and soft mushroom-grey coat and the grey stone-smooth head but she stayed small. Nevertheless, this little dog, following her running master on his training regimes, became a giant in the sport. She ran where Chris ran, no questions asked, rain, sun and cold.

Chris' mother-in-law, fondly known as Maudie to Chris, worried about the "poor wee doggie" running in such cold winter weather. She made Frodo a wool coat. Of course the dog didn't want to put it on. But Maudie would persevere, shoving Frodo's legs through the holes and buttoning up the front in spite of the dog's protests—a struggle between two independent beings.

Jasper, the friendly male black Labrador, was part of the family long before Frodo, but he had to get used to sharing life with Frodo. Of course Frodo was the boss and Jasper often had to play second dog. They were an interesting team. When someone came into the yard—a letter carrier, perhaps—Jasper would provide the appropriate big bark. That would distract the person. Meanwhile the real threat was Frodo. She was heading straight for the ankles.

One night, Maudie's good friend Christine came over for supper. Christine was very proper in her person and in her ways. Frodo was just the opposite. She would get excited and even somewhat aggressive when company came. As a result, when Christine visited, Maudie would put Frodo in a bedroom and close the door so that Christine would be unbothered by the dog. But a short time into this particular visit, Maudie forgot that Frodo was still locked in the room. She inadvertently opened the door and out raced Frodo. The dog was in super shape so she came out growling and racing at high speed, leaping onto the chair and coming dangerously close to Christine's throat. Undoubtedly, Christine's heart was racing as she blurted, "My goodness Maude, what a vicious dog."

Chris' Maudie died at the end of July, 2009 after a long and happy life. She was in her 103rd year. Chris wrote the following message to Marie.

Thank you for informing me about your mother's passing. I hope
she went as quietly and peacefully as she deserved. I have thought
of her frequently with great fondness. She was always so wonderful
to me, and I shall never forget her bond with Frodo. I have many
great memories of scones in the kitchen and days at Gimli.

Yes, Chris was one of Maudie's favourites—second only to Frodo. She
could get away with almost anything, including being boss dog to Jasper.

After several years of study, Chris decided that a career in psychology was not for him. In the summer of 1972, Chris assumed the position
of recreation director for a summer program for children in Gimli. He
enjoyed the work and especially the interaction with children. Here was
an alternate career path. Chris was destined for teaching.

By the end of 1972, Chris and Marie decided to go their separate
ways. The marriage ended—an amicable parting.

In September, 1973, Chris enrolled in the Early Childhood
Certification Programme, Faculty of Education, University of Manitoba.
Upon graduation, he signed a contract in June, 1974 with the Winnipeg
School Division. He began teaching in fall, 1974 at Kent Road School.

Throughout these years, as a result of his running and coaching for
the track team at the University of Manitoba, Chris had met a core of
dedicated runners. He had a new running goal—to compete for Canada
in the 1976 Montreal Olympics. His fellow runners from the University
of Manitoba were with him on the challenge. They were invaluable in
the course of his training: competing with him, encouraging him, and
providing an essential camaraderie.

CHRIS' DIARY, 2009

March 1 Last night I wrote "The Yellow River" by I P Freely, eliminated 3.9 litres between midnight and 6 a.m. I lost 4.2 kg. Feel
much better today—not bloaty abdomen, more relaxed, had some
dreams last night.

March 18 Oksana came in to tell us bone marrow biopsy on for
9:30 am tomorrow.

March 23 Continuing to sleep longer between pee breaks...
Dr. Kumar came by to talk about results; no apparent leukemia,
too few blast cells to be sure—another biopsy in a week.

March 25 First full day at home

March 26 Home day 2. Up at 7:30 am, 16-minute stair-walk while
pancakes cooking, blueberry pancakes.

April 1 Daly and Towns over for visit 10:30—11:40. Grant brought
shrimp/noodles and green beans. Had shrimp for lunch, very
good, went for nap—did 31 minute walk outside.

April 3 Called Mom, happy birthday

April 19 Sue and I discussed getting married

April 20 Read over stem cell transplant info. (pretty upsetting side
effect potential)

April 24 Arrived Enid around 4:30 visit/Mom, Rilla, Marvin

Olympian Dreams

WITH THE FUTURE 1976 OLYMPIC GOAL IN MIND, CHRIS WOULD SPEND more time on the 5-km and 10-km races and the cross country competitions. On November 16, 1974, he competed in the Canadian cross country championships at Brock University in St. Catharines, Ontario. This was an open 12,000-metre run. Neil Cusak of Ireland won the race with a time of 33:23.2 and Chris placed fourth at 34:17.

On November 30, 1974, Chris ran at the American Athletic Association National Cross Country meet in Belmont, California. He and Larry Switzer were the only competitors from the Canadian Track & Field Association. Chris placed 18th of 270 runners with a time of 31:05.9. The winning time of John Ngeno of Washington State University was 29:58.8.

On June 19, 1975, Chris won the 5.4-mile open road race at Kenora, Ontario with a time of 25:26. His running partners, Sheldon Reynolds and Karl Sproll, were second and third.

ON JUNE 30, 1975, CHRIS COMPLETED HIS FIRST YEAR OF TEACHING. He'd had a good year. There was a young and exuberant staff, lots of freedom to try new things in the classroom and a school far enough from his home for a good workout running or bicycling.

His Kent Road teaching colleague Mavis Riley recalled how much Chris enjoyed interacting with students and how they responded.

> He loved to read to the kids. They would rush to gather around—pushing and jostling as Grade 2's must—as he announced, "kids—we've got a great story for you today."

But, he went beyond normal classroom activities. This was a time of popularity of disco dancing and Chris was right into it. He held early morning pre-school dance classes where both teachers and students participated. That was a great way to start the day.

At Kent Road School, finding a comfortable reading environment might have been the reason why he and his Grade 2 colleague, Rosemary Krushel, convinced principal John Buchanan that they needed three classrooms and not two. The extra room had a soft carpet ideal for sitting cross-legged and reading to his second-grade charges. Chris loved to read poetry and I can imagine him reciting Dennis Lee's piece—

"Alligator pie, alligator pie,
If I don't get some I think I'm gonna die.
Give away the green grass, give away the sky,
But don't give away my alligator pie"

Other days he would read from Aesop's Fables or perhaps a piece from Bill Martin Jr.'s "The Little Squeegy Bug", "Trick or Treat?" or "Caddie the Golf Dog". This activity was critical for opening up student minds to the world of literature.

Chris wanted students to have fun at school—to learn in a non-competitive setting and to be recognized for all sorts of achievements. In this spirit, Rosemary and Chris created a special toque called Noodles. If a student did something worthy of praise, the reward was Noodles—around the neck or on the head. If you did something extra special, you might even get to take Noodles home. Noodles became synonymous with recognition—a pat on the back for meeting a challenge, for attaining a goal or for just doing the right thing—and at some point during the year every student earned the privilege.

Realizing that teachers need to establish control in the class, Chris tried a time-out form of discipline—removing bad behaviour from an adoring audience. He had a manner that was so loving and accepting as to what each student could do.

Chris was a non-confrontational person but highly principled. He wasn't afraid to stand up for causes he believed in. In his early years, he encountered a very bright autistic student. The parents were planning to move the pupil to a specialized autistic program. Chris was of the belief that everyone could be integrated into the public system and he argued that the proper environment could be created to make the child comfortable and to challenge his intellect.

There was another instance when Chris disagreed with a parental decision. It wasn't confrontational but Chris was stating his case. The child was gifted and had shown achievement. As a result the parents were lobbying to have the student bumped to a higher grade. Chris made the point that academia is never the whole story. If bumped up, the child would have to adapt to a room of older students and was she mature enough to meet this challenge? Would the effects of that disruption eliminate the benefits of the potential higher level of learning? Undoubtedly, Chris was thinking of his own situation—youngest in the class—and the challenges that created for him.

The slower reader never knew that he or she was a slow reader. Chris and Rosemary would continually form new reading groups and the child needing extra help would get it—without fanfare.

Chris developed a physical education program for the Kindergarten to grade three students. There were stations of activity, including folk dancing. Chris convinced the Grade 6 students to set up the stations prior to class.

Chris, Rosemary, Mavis and others organized an overnight campout for the Grades 1-3 students—some 120 of them. The children went home after school on the Friday and then came back an hour or so later. Mavis recalls the highlights of the occasion.

> The children were divided into small groups—each with an adult in charge. We couldn't have done this without the parent volunteers. We started off the evening with a barbecue and outdoor games, lots of fun and lots of noise. Then there were late night snacks and quiet activities—campfire songs and stories. Each little group bedded down around the walls of the gym. Needless to say, sleep was

the last thing on the minds of the children but we did eventually get everyone settled for a few hours of slumber. Next morning the volunteer cooking-parents made a pancake breakfast. It was a great experience for all.

Could it get any better for these primary learners?

Kent Road principal, John A. Buchanan, in his report on probationary first year teacher Chris McCubbins, was also impressed with Chris' performance. Here are some of his words.

> Mr. McCubbins has become a valued member of the Kent Road team. He has developed a remarkable rapport with the primary pupils. The primary Phys. Ed. Program has been greatly improved through his work...his first year has been outstandingly successful.

Teaching colleague Rosemary provides a succinct description of teacher Chris.

> Chris lived what he did. He didn't just go to work.

CHRIS HAD BEEN TRAINING HARD IN THE 5-KM AND 10-KM DISTANCES. In May, 1975, he posted a 29:24.6 time in the 10-km. In June he ran the 5-km in 14:24.2. Then in July at the Pan Am Stadium, he ran the 3000-metre steeplechase in the Manitoba track & field championships. He placed first with a time of 8:51.8. Undoubtedly, Chris was keeping his options open for the upcoming Olympic trials in Montreal.

Runner Sheldon Reynolds provided an apt description of Chris' running style.

> Chris was an endurance runner. He would try to set a hard pace in the middle of the race to break the end-of-race sprinters (i.e. the kickers like Yifter the Shifter.) Holding a good speed throughout the race could break the spirit of some runners. The truth was that no one in Manitoba could stay with Chris—he was that strong.

The Canadian Open Olympic trials were held at Kent Park in Montreal on July 25, 1975. Chris ran a great race in the 10,000-metre with tough competition from Miruts Yifter of Ethiopia. Chris' time was 28:16.51—a sixth-place finish but a record-breaking Canadian time.

Here's how Chris described his race in his running diary of July 24 and 25—no fanfare, no bragging, just the facts.

RUNNING DIARY

> *Thursday July 24* 10 miles, flew to Montreal got to bed about 12:30
> *Friday July 25* AM @18 degrees, 20-30 mph, cloudy
> Od. 28 min easy
> PM @20 degrees, 20-30 mph cloudy
> Od. Jog, strides, jogging-striding-stretching
> Raced 10,000 metre—28:16.51 placed 6th, Yifter (Ethiopia 1st),
>   jogged and back to housing
> About 13:35 at 12 laps

For those (like myself) who have never kept a running diary, there is a need to explain. As a warm-up on the Friday morning, Chris does a 28-minute workout—outdoors (Od.). That night, again (Od.) he warms up with a jog, some quicker short runs (strides), then some quicker short runs with jogging between (jogging strides). The 13:35 is a measure of his time at 12 laps or the three mile mark—nearly one-half way through the race.

Years later, Chris commented on how much he enjoyed this record-setting Montreal race.

> Montreal was a smash when I broke the standard in the 10,000. We
> had about a dozen guys within a few yards of each other all the way.
> I love a race like that.

His run set a Manitoban native record for the 10,000-metre race. The record was still standing as of early 2013.

This was a very close race with the elite of international runners. It placed Chris as one of the top ten fastest men in the world in the

10,000-metre race. Yifter came on strong on the last few laps for a first place time of 28:09.14. It was a typical win for Yifter the Shifter.

Miruts Yifter was a talented long-distance runner with a unique ability to turn it on in the late stages of a race. He had a trademark "spring-apart" leap that he displayed in the last few laps of a race. Thus, he was tagged as the "shifter". Miruts would shift into this new gear, gain a quick lead and hold it to win the race.

Yifter loved to run and won 221 of the 252 races in his competitive running career. As it turned out, Ethiopia boycotted the 1976 Olympics. Yifter was back with his end-of-race acceleration for the Moscow games in 1980 to win gold medals in both the 5000-metre and 10,000-metre races. What energy and tenacity he had—breaking free of the pack in the last minutes of a long-distance race to win.

As Sheldon Reynolds explained, Chris didn't do this kind of spurt. Instead, he would grind out a win, trying to crush the guys in the middle of a race so they didn't have anything left at the end.

Chris was surely enjoying the game in 1975. He was not only running well and winning races but also enjoying the company and success of his running companions. On August 12, Chris and the team travelled to Regina for the Western Canada Summer Games. As his running colleagues would agree, it didn't matter to Chris if he was up against world-famous harriers such as Yifter the Shifter or against friends with whom he trained.

The meet organizers in Regina decided to give one gold medal to the most exceptional athlete of the meet and certificates of participation to everyone else—a departure from the normal protocol. Chris won the gold for his times of 8:59 in the 3000-metre steeplechase and 14:12.2 in the 5000-metre race—both firsts. He won against some serious competition. In the end, it was a tight race in the 5000-metre. Tom Howard finished second at 14:32.2 and Ken French third at 14:40. It was again the kind of run that Chris loved—few strides separating the finishers. Chris followed Howard for a good portion of the race and then broke away for the remaining laps. In an interview with Al Besson, *Winnipeg Free Press* staff writer ("He Runs With A Flare—That's Chris' Torch," August 14, 1975), Chris, with his signature brand of humour, had the following take on his strategy of following Tom Howard closely as a wind break for three-quarters of the race.

> I stayed with Howard for nine and a half laps and when he didn't accept my challenge then, I broke for the finish. I feel very bad about that though. I used him to break the wind for me almost all the way. I don't like to do that to a nice person like him. We're friends.

The rest of the Manitoban team also performed well. For example, Sheldon Reynolds was fifth at 15:16.8 and Grant Towns sixth at 16:24.2. At the end of the meet when the gold medal winner was announced, Chris' teammates gave him a miniature Canadian flag to accompany his gold medal and his victory run. He was ecstatic. Of all the meets in which he had competed—from Provo to Glasgow to the Winnipeg Pan Am to the worlds in Montreal—and all the top-class runners he had competed against, to Chris, winning in Regina was just as important. As friend Sheldon observed:

> He was waving the small Manitoba flag jogging a victory lap and grinning like a Cheshire cat!!

Dale Eisler of *The Regina Leader Post* ("Manitoban Makes Move," p. 22, August 14, 1975) wrote about how the crowd of near 4000 fans loved Chris' run in the steeplechase and loved him even more for his win in the 5000-metre. He ran victory laps for both races and afterwards included the following quote from Chris.

> They paid their money to get in and I like to put on a show if I can. When there's a crowd I like to let them know I appreciate it. You got to have fans. It isn't fun running when there isn't anyone watching.

On August 22-24, 1975, the Canadian National Track and Field Championships were held in Sudbury, Ontario. Chris was fresh off a record time in the 10-km and was anxious to make his presence known to Canadian runners. He wanted to do well in these championships, and was disappointed with the results—a third-place showing and a time of

29:25.2. Unusually for him, the pace he set early on in the race was too fast. His running diary tells the story.

RUNNING DIARY
> *August 22* @ +15C, 15mph, sunny od. 28 min easy
> PM @ +23C, 10-15mph, sunny
> Od. Jogged, strides, jogging/strides,
> 10,000 metre 29:25.2—3rd place
> Got ball of gas in stomach
> 4:30, 9:02, 13:39 bad lap no idea pace
> Jog a little maybe 2 mi

In this entry, Chris lists the split times—4:30 for 1 mile, 9:02 for 2 miles and 13:39 for 3 miles.

The phrase "jog a little" referred to the cool down at the end of the race. Sheldon Reynolds, who also participated in this race, ran with Chris for the cool-down. It was far from a quiet jog. Chris was hammering, desperate to clear the memory of his mistake.

Four days later, on August 26, Chris ran the 3000-metre race in Sudbury and set a Manitoba native record-breaking time of 8:09.2.

In spite of the rigour and time commitment of preparing for the '76 Olympics, Chris still had time for some fun with his Manitoban running mates. Such an opportunity arose on September 14, 1975. Karl Sproll described the occasion.

> A race was organized to see how far you could run in one hour. This was a novelty and the runners were hyped about it—enthralled by the notion of setting a record. Chris on the other hand was as cool and collected as ever. He was calculating the pace that he would need to run in order to maximize his distance, and of course he won, covering 19,177 metres or 11 miles, 1612 yards.

Suppliers of sports equipment would often provide running gear for elite athletes. It was an opportunity to test the equipment. In the summer of 1975, Chris received new shoes with spikes. There was very little support in the shoes but Chris trained in them on the indoor track through the first two weeks of September. Due to vigorous training and the lack of support in the shoes, Chris suffered a stress fracture in his foot. He was out of action from mid-September through to the end of October. Chris was concerned about his lack of conditioning, since he was entered in the Canadian Cross Country Championships in Vancouver on November 15, and planned on fulfilling that commitment.

His first serious run was on October 18 in a local four-mile cross-country run. He came in first with a time of 22:11. As his running diary attests, he felt tentative after such a long layoff.

RUNNING DIARY

First attempt, felt pretty good, foot seemed o.k. a little tender [tired] after—afraid to really push, arch seems to be fatiguing.

Running partner Karl Sproll was also entered in the Cross Country Championships in Vancouver. Karl boarded the plane in Winnipeg the day prior to the race en-route to Vancouver and got seated—to his surprise—next to Grant McLaren. McLaren was one of the elite Ontario cross-country runners. He was the defending champion and a very strong competitor. The topic of conversation moved to Chris. What kind of shape was he in? Was he running well?

Karl told him the truth. Chris was in horrible condition. He had these bad spikes and had fractured his foot. Subsequently, he had been out of action for six weeks. The news was soon to be verified. When Karl and Grant landed in Vancouver, they took the taxi to the Hotel Vancouver. Upon entering the lobby, they saw Chris slouched in a big leather chair. Folded over, with his legs in the fetal position, he looked bad—his hair was drooping, and his eyes were foggy.

Karl said, "Chris, are you O.K.?" And Chris replied, "I'm feeling horrible—I'm really sick."

The race took place the next day in Stanley Park. There were 72 runners—the who's who of Canadian cross country. For the first mile or so, Chris was running with Karl in the middle of the pack. And then, he decided to move on—winding his way through the maze of runners.

There was a hill up ahead and Karl and the rest of the Manitoban contingent were trying to pick out Chris in the herd. They spotted him moving up the hill, approaching the leaders of the race. Then once Chris was over the top, the rest of the Manitoban runners lost track of him for the rest of the race.

When Karl arrived at the finish line, he saw Chris and shouted, "How did you do?" "I won," said Chris in his nonchalant manner. "Wow, how did you do it?" "Those guys just quit running," said Chris, grinning ear to ear.

Chris had a winning time of 37:28.4 for the 12,000-metre run. A close race, with past champion Grant McLaren in second place at 37:42.4

Here's Chris' running diary account for the race.

RUNNING DIARY

November 15 A.M. +7C, calm, cloudy

Od. 40 min (easy jog) a couple strides, National X-Country, 12,000 metres, 1st 37:28.4, 3-mile jog, mostly gravel track/roads, fell about 4 mi—no mileage marks.

Then, after his return to Winnipeg:

RUNNING DIARY

Sunday Nov 16 felt really bent—tendon areas felt pounded from hard surfaces

Chris' right tendon, his right Achilles sheath and his lower-right calf were sore after the national cross country meet. He visited trainer Scotty McVickar who advised him "to lay off for a few days." Nevertheless, Chris still ran 15 miles in spite of his "bent" feelings. Undoubtedly, he was thinking "A two-day layoff, don't be crazy. The guys on the line next to me are working hard today and I'm sitting idle. That can't be a good strategy."

Chris ended 1975 with a race on December 30 in Saskatoon. Here's his take.

RUNNING DIARY

> 2 mile placed 2nd 8:46, 4:20 at mile 6:31 at 1.5 miles, didn't feel like I slowed—a bit tight in back, didn't feel too bad—lead from mi—1.5 miles. Very poor night's sleep.

Chris would become a Canadian in 1976 and was planning a serious run at the '76 Olympics in Montreal.

CHRIS, JUNE 7, 2009

I did manage to achieve total remission from the treatment (March 23). Because of the pneumonia it took several weeks for me to recover enough to undergo consolidation treatment. During the recovery time we were able to go to visit my mom in Enid (April 24). Upon returning from Enid the doctor scheduled me to begin consolidation in early May. I started on a Monday. The doctor did a marrow biopsy that day. He called the next day to tell us the leukemia had returned and I already had over 30% blast cells in my biopsy. As a result I re-entered HSC on May 6 for a second round of induction therapy. I was discharged from HSC on June 2 having reached official remission with about 5% blast cells. During the last induction session my tongue developed sores and became swollen. I was on a blender and Ensure diet for almost a week. I managed to maintain my weight.

My siblings were tested to see if any of them were a 10 for 10 stem cell match for me. They look at the DNA on one of the chromosomes in the immune system. Fortunately, both Tip and Rilla match me. Rilla who has been here for over 3 weeks helping us has already undergone further testing to see if she would be appropriate. Tip arrives later today and will begin further testing Monday. The hope is that Tip will be the donor because we are the same sex and Rilla has had children. They are checking the blood to see if there are any hidden viruses that could infect me after the transplant.

I re-enter the hospital on Thursday and begin more chemo on Friday to prepare me for the transplant. The donor begins getting neupogen shots to stimulate stem cell release from their bones at that time. The process is timed so I end chemo when the hospital harvests stem cells from the donor. The day after harvesting the stem cells they are given to me through a central line which I will have installed tomorrow.

After the chemo and transplant I will face the potential of several different side effects. Some are due to the chemo and others are due to the host versus graft effect. Host—Graft is basically my bone marrow and the donor's stem cells fighting for control of my body. We are of course rooting for the donors to win and kill off the leukemia in me.

If all goes well I should be out of hospital in 4-6 weeks but have several months of an immune system that is very depressed and general weakness. The hope is that I will have several years to a full life of remission. The doctors in this area actually do not talk of cure until the patient has died of some other cause. As you can imagine we have been on a huge emotional roller coaster.

We have certainly learned the importance of looking at the beauty in every day. Enjoy and Smile.

CHRIS' DIARY, 2009

May 4 Started consolidation chemo today. Had bone marrow biopsy from Dr. Kumar

May 5 Out of remission (35% blast) pretty hard shock...talked about long term if no transplant match, very upsetting afternoon and evening, need to get refocused.

May 6 Met Dr. David Schwitzer one of Dr. Team. Told us only 40% of patients my age achieve second remission (Real shot to gut).

May 15 Best sleep I've had. Win was not a match but Tip is.

May 19 Pastor Phil arrived, he went to retreat room, Sue, Rilla, Marvin arrived, Marvin joined Phil, Rilla joined them. Sue and I changed clothes, sat together then went across the hall to get married. After Phil left, Marvin and Rilla stayed for a little while.

May 28 If in remission, transplant 10-14 days after, relaxed, Dr. Kumar came by, talked about plan, if in remission on June 3 transplant target June 13, Tip should arrive for June 7

June 2 waiting for bone marrow results… Dr. Rubinger finally came in around 3:30 with results 5.2% blasts. Plan is for chemo for transplant to begin June 15.

June 3 to Assiniboine Park, to watch Run/Walk for GD6, good crowd, lots of friends in walk/run and helping. Pretty emotional evening—had to keep people away to avoid germs.

1976 Olympics Year

1976 WAS THE YEAR OF THE MONTREAL OLYMPIC GAMES. EARLY IN THE year, Chris realized that funding to support his training for the games would only happen if he belonged to a registered running club. He had been running informally with a group of friends from the University of Manitoba and enjoyed their camaraderie. In late January, this group met to plan registration of their informal running group. A name was all they needed to make it formal. There were lots of possibilities but Chris liked "Yellow Snow." It was another chance to snub one's nose at officialdom— to have some fun—running under the radar of the established clubs. On February 2, 1976, the Yellow Snow Track Club was officially registered.

There was one other matter that needed attention, a crucial matter if Chris was planning to run for Canada. He had to become a Canadian citizen. Application was made in early January and a hearing for a Certificate of Canadian Citizenship was scheduled for March 24.

In the spring of 1976, the *Winnipeg Free Press* ran an article titled "Olympics Elusive for McCubbins, But He's Healthy this Year". It presented the following take on Chris' past injuries.

McCubbins has been the victim of the fickle finger of fate as far as Olympics are concerned for the past two games.

In 1968 he broke a leg and was kept off the U.S. team that went to Mexico, and in 1972 an Achilles tendon injury stopped him from going to Munich.

"I'm just waiting for something to happen this year," he quipped.

At the moment he is taking it easy as he has been plagued for a few weeks with a strained hip.

"I was doing well up until two weeks ago. I still run up to 20 miles a day, but don't do it quite as fast. I'd like to get moving again."

There were also some words from Chris on his diet and strategy when running.

"I stick to healthy foods, but I'm not a health food fanatic. I did try a vegetarian diet one winter, but it was just out of curiosity, I found it was too hard to maintain, especially when you travel. You go into one restaurant and your diet is shot.

I don't really have any strategy in mind when I enter a race, I don't even care who I'm racing against.

A lot of people plot out a race. They decide how they'll run against one guy and how they'll run against another. Lots of times these guys don't show up, or they do something different. I just play it by ear."

On February 14 in Winnipeg, Chris ran in the 3000-metre race at the Knights of Columbus Indoor Games. It was a competitive field with Ron Martin of Great Britain coming first at 8:02.0 and Joshua Kimeto of Kenya second at 8:11.0. Chris was third at 8:17 but encountered an incident on the track.

RUNNING DIARY
    i.d. 2mi. Strides, 3000 metre 8:17, 3rd, 2 mi jog. Tripped by pole vault official 1st lap, Caught up—died—Arms tired (66, 2:10, 3:16, 4:22, 5:26, 6:35)

The 3000-metre race is less than two miles. Chris kept track of his split times—66 seconds for the 1/4 mile, 2 minutes 10 seconds for the 1/2 mile, 3:16 for 3/4 mile, 4:22 for the mile, 5:26 for 1.25 miles, 6:35 for 1.5 miles.

In March 1976, Chris got time off from the Winnipeg School Division to train. He was going to be competing in the Drake Relays in April, so he went to Flagstaff, Arizona for training. Flagstaff is at a higher altitude and, being a disciple of Jack Daniels, he thought that this would be an opportunity to increase his oxygen intake. An unexpected spring storm dumped lots of snow, so training at Flagstaff was cancelled. He headed to Enid, Oklahoma to continue his training at the familiar grounds of the OSU track. There was the added bonus of visiting with family and friends in Enid. Then he moved on to California and higher-altitude training near San Francisco. Conveniently, his sister Rilla and family lived in San Anselmo, another good reason for choosing the surrounding hills as a training site. Prior to leaving Enid, he was interviewed by Wayne Bunch of the *Enid News Eagle*. Chris reflected on staying in Canada and running in the Olympics for a different country.

> ...I decided to stay in Canada. I like the political and social atmosphere. I've lived there for five years now and you give some commitment to a country in that period of time.
>
> They don't feel like I'm trying to sneak into the Olympics. Besides, I don't think you run for a country. Basically, a runner runs for himself.
>
> You're the one doing all the work and taking the pain. So, you just run for yourself.

On April 1 and 2, Chris ran the 10-km and 5-km in Austin, Texas. His respective times were 29:01.2 and 13:55.64. His running diary with his placement and interval times told the story.

RUNNING DIARY
April 1 +75 F, 5 mph, sunny
Od. 2 mi jog, strides, 10,000 m 29:01.2, 3rd (72, 2:23, 3:30, 4:38, 9:09, 13:52, 28:04) felt really heavy about 4.5 miles—felt pretty heavy last 1.5 miles.

For the above 10,000-metre race, Chris is keeping track of his interval times: 72 seconds for 1/4mile; 2:23 minutes for 1/2mile; 3:30 minutes for 3/4mile; and 4:38 for the mile; 9:09 for 2 miles; 13:52 for 3 miles and 28:04 for 6 miles. The 10,000-metre is longer than six miles (by some

375 yards or 346 metres), so another partial turn of the track results in a final time of 29:01.2.

> *April 2* 65—70 F. 5-10 mph, clear od. 2mi jog, strides, jog, 5000 metre, 13:55.64 2nd , 2 mi jog
> Felt lousy warming up, pretty good in race.
> (68, 2:15, 3:23, 4:30, 5:38, 6:45 +, 7:55, 9:05, 10:14, 11:23, 12:27, 13:28+)

For the 5000-metre race, Chris is again keeping track of his interval times—fractions of a mile and miles. He is 4:30 for the mile; 9:05 for 2 miles and 13:28+ for 3 miles. The 5000 metre race is some 126 metres longer than the 3-mile. Thus, the finishing time of 13:55.64 reflects this extra distance.

On April 24, Chris ran the 10-km at the Drake Relays in Des Moines, Iowa. It was another close race—the type that Chris loved. The standard for the race was 28:40 and the first four runners beat the standard. Ed Mendoza was first at 28:13.15. Chris was fourth at 28:28.0. It was like the Montreal race of the previous summer—a tight contest to the end.

He was focused on the Olympic Games, but his joy of running still shone through. The fun of being in a race was always more important to him than time or place.

Chris also ran a personal best in the 5000-metre race at the Drake meet. His time was 13:51.8. Chris' best times in these races were 28:16.0 in the 10,000-metre and 13:44 in the 5000-metre.There is an evaluation table that translates these times to one mile equivalents. His 10,000-metre time is equal to a 3:51 mile and his 5000 to a 3:55 mile. Here are the running diaries for the Drake Relays.

RUNNING DIARY

> *April 23* Drake Relays, Des Moines, Iowa '60 F, 5-10 mph, overcast—2 mi jog, strides, 5000 m @ 13:51.8 (2nd place—3 mi or 4828 metres @ 13:22) "never got loose, no zip" (67, 2:15, 3:21, 4:26, 6:42, 8:57, 10:02, 11:08, 12:15, 13:22) 'very heavy'

April 24 2nd day of the Drake Relays 10,000 metres 4th at 28:28.6.
6 miles (or 9656 m) 27:32.4 "really heavy today."
(66, 2:15.5, 3:24, 4:33, 5:41, 6:46, 7:55, 9:05, 10:14, 11:23.9, 12:33,
13:41, 14:51, 16:00, 17:09, 18:18, 19:27, 20:37, 21:48, 22:58,
24:06, 25:16, 26:24, 27:33)

The underlined times from the above entry are the one-mile through six-mile times.

On May 8 in Knoxville, Tennessee, Chris ran the 5000-metre in the Tom Black Classic meet. Mike Keogh of the New York Athletic Club won with a track-record time of 13:39.1. Another close race with Chris second at 13:44—a time also good enough to beat the track record.

RUNNING DIARY

May 8 Tom Black Classic, 5000 m.
50F, 5 mph, cloudy, od. 40 min. Jog around Ed's farm (Mom's brother), felt horrible all day—sore throat. O.d. 2 mi jog, strides, jogging strides (stomach very crampy) 5000 m @ 13:44.8 (2nd), 2 mi jog, (66, 2:12, 3:18, 4:23, 8:48, 11:03, 13:17) no motivation
Lap times 66, 66, 66, 65, 311, 135, 134

The Canadian Olympic Trials were held in Laval Quebec on May 29 & 30. Chris placed first in the 10,000-metre and third in the 5000-metre.

RUNNING DIARY

May 29 Olympic Trials '25 C, 15–20 mph, light overcast, od. 2 mi jog, strides, 10000 m @ 29:29, 1st, 14:25 @ 5000 lapped all but Skawani? Broke away at 2.5 mi, got stitch, felt dead

One day after this race, Chris was stepping off a curb and appeared to land the wrong way. Although he ran well in the 5000-metre the next day, this freak misstep appeared as the genesis of a groin injury recorded in the following May 30 entry.

RUNNING DIARY

> *May 30* +26C, 15-20 mph, sunny
> Od. 2 mi jog, strides - 5000 metres @ 14:27. 3rd
> To 1.5 miles o.k. then could care less, no speed, groin a bit tender

Rest was now called for to heal the groin injury but Chris was convinced that rest was for the weak, and this was not the time to slack off. He was in the best shape of his running career and he wasn't about to let it slip. Toiling and pushing through the pain was his preferred option.

He returned to Winnipeg and struggled with training up to the time of the Olympic Games. The following running diary provides a glimpse into the extent and severity of his injuries and his determination to run—irrespective of the message of his body pains.

RUNNING DIARY—JUNE-JULY '76

After his first easy 15-mile run on May 31/76, Chris felt

> "absolutely horrid, right groin sore!"

> *June 1* Dr. McVickar –"groin strain! Right groin sore, left hip sore, back tight, felt dead, off balance running. McVickar says try it?
> *June 2* "groin very sore—hips a bit"

But Chris still ran 111 miles that week.

In the week of June 3–9, Chris consulted with a chiropractor and continued treatment with Dr. McVickar. On June 9 he had run 83 miles for the week but

> "groin still bugging me. Not going to Montreal"

Except for June 15 when Chris wrote

> "groin still keeping me down'"

Generally for the week of June 10–16

> "the groin feeling better."

He ran 133 miles for the week.

June 17–23 In general, the comments are that
"the groin is feeling better this week."

On the 22nd, he did
"6 x 880 intervals @ (2:09, 2:08, 2:05, 2:06, 2:07 and 2:06)"

June 22 "left groin & hip tightened up afterward—could feel it
some during 880m, body felt good."

June 23 He did an easy, very slow 2-mi jog and finished the week at
121 mi. But
"couldn't run, leg-groin extremely painful—leg very bad, light swim."

He did ride his bicycle to school.

June 24–30 Groin feeling bad at the beginning of the week and by the 29th
"feeling better, maybe there is hope!"

He cycled every day—ran 52 miles for the week.

July 1 ass & right hamstring really sore & crampy—after 6.5 miles—
scrapped evening run. Very depressed.

July 5 Flew to Montreal after a 5-mile easy run, then did an outdoor
run for 65 minutes.
"Saw more physio—not sure groin strain, increased nerve or her-
nia, 2 doctors, several physio."
July 6 Decided for sure strained groin!—3 more doctors more
physios—second hydro-cortisone injection. No running for 48
hours!
July 7 More physio, pain more localized—intense—spent about 6
hrs at physio.
July 8 4 sessions of physio leg still sore' od. 2 mi easy jog. leg still
sore also hip from tapping (2 miles)
July 9 another cortisone injection in three spots of groin area, shit! (o)

July 10 getting better (o)
July 11 seems to be improving (o)
July 12 'tomorrow I get to jog (o)'

July 13 He jogged 3 miles in the morning and 3 in the afternoon
"easy, leg sore worse in afternoon—5 sessions at physio"
July 14 Jogged for 30 min (easy) and did 4+ miles leg and groin
getting better

July 15-21 This week he did 35 miles of easy jogging in the morning and 33 miles of workout in the afternoon for a weekly total of 68. Here are the daily comments.

July 15 feeling about the same as yesterday groin /butt still sore.
July 16 groin better right butt pretty sore
July 17 leg sore, Opening Ceremonies, leg really bad!
July 18 Tried some fartlek (Bad!)

Fartlek is a Swedish training technique done on trails and parks and interpreted as "speed play." Chris liked this exercise. For example, he would run hard "to the park bench" and then jog to the "road crossing" then run hard again to the "large clump of evergreens" and then jog to the "burnt patch of grass." It is generally a transition type of workout done from pre-season to more rigorous interval training. In this case, the groin muscles were flaring.

July 19 Cortisone shot, 30 min jog 4+, then another 4+ in the afternoon, felt better
July 20 did 10 miles jogging
July 21 Did intervals: 6x10 metre acc, 6x20 metre acc, 4x50 metre acc, 4x100 metre acc, 5 min jog. leg felt good running a bit tight afterward.
July 22 In afternoon, od. 15 min easy, stretch, 25 min jog butt and abductor tight—sore, groin felt o.k. (5mi)

The day of the Olympics 10,000-metre heat

July 23 Stayed in race for about 2400 metres, groin began hurting
at 1200 metres, everything hurt by finish—headache possible
heat exhaustion?
27 C, 10 mph, sunny
Od. 10-15 min. Jog, stretching, strides, jogging,
10,000 m heat Olympic Games, 12th 33:22.35
Never felt anything so bad before! Had to go for dope test! Irony!
An hour to walk home.
July 24 Sore everywhere—feel like I ran a double marathon—can
hardly walk.
No More Running until 100%. Maybe September?

Chris' coach and mentor Jack Daniels had watched the race. Jack was
working for CBC Sports as a colour commentator for the modern pentathlon event. He felt that many people wouldn't know that Chris had
run most of the race in one of the outer lanes of the track in order not
to get in the way of those who were fit and racing well and eventually
may be lapping Chris in the race. Daniels figured there were two things
going on in Chris' mind. First, he knew he was not ready to race and
he didn't want to mess up anyone else's race. In some of the other races,
slow runners had not moved over and got in the way of contenders—
and in several cases had prevented that runner from making it to the
final. Secondly, he didn't want to let Canada down by not running the
race. It had nothing to do with how he felt about or for himself. Being a
poor sport and impeding the race of another runner and not honouring
his obligation as a Canadian athlete would be the last things that Chris
McCubbins would ever want to do.

Typically, Chris wasn't making any excuses for this race—no different from any others where he didn't live up to his own expectations.
But his friends and a prominent Canadian broadcaster knew the truth
of his injuries.

Canadian CBC radio host Peter Gzowski was in the stands the day
of the Olympic race. He was amazed at Chris' tenacity in finishing—not

dropping out in spite of the inevitable pain of his injuries. He was in contact with Chris after the race and sent him the tape of his *Morningside* broadcast. Here are some excerpts from the transcription of the tape.

There was a moment yesterday when I wanted to stand up in my observer's station at the Olympic stadium and yell at the 70,000 or so people who were there watching the first day of track and field.

"He's hurting," I wanted to yell, "he's in agony. He shouldn't even be in this race and what he's going through deserves at least as much applause and support as you are giving the leaders"—that's what I wanted to yell.

And the 'he' I wanted to yell about is Chris McCubbins. McCubbins is a former steeple-chaser and a former American who now runs the 10,000 metres for Canada—or at least used to run it.

He might, I suppose, quit now. He's thirty-one years old and he's eliminated from these games.

He finished 12th in his heat won by a Portuguese named Lopez and keep your eye on him when the finals start in which only the first four finishers qualified to stay in.

And McCubbins finished five full minutes over his best time. Lopez won the heat in 28:04. In other competitions this year McCubbins has run as quickly as 28:16.

And people who know him say that just before these games began he was in better shape than he'd ever been. Was that is. Until in practice in Winnipeg just three weeks ago, he pulled a groin muscle.

Pulled groins are like back injuries or like the gout. They sound kind of amusing but until you've had them you don't know how much they hurt and it's hard to think of an event that a pulled groin could hurt more in than the 10,000-metre run.

Lopez and a lot of other people lapped McCubbins at least 4 times yesterday...but he finished.

He finished.

He has—say those who know him—too much pride not too. Pride—that's something people don't talk about much here at these games, but it's an essential part of them. These competitors have worked hard and long just to get here through local meets, regional meets, national trials—competitions against the clock to meet international standards.

The display that Chris McCubbins put on yesterday—a display that was virtually unnoticed by a crowd that seemed to be cheering more for Americans than winners in that order—than for Canadians—typifies an athlete's pride as much as anything I've seen here so far.

A lot of people came here with a special eye on him. There is—in a location I won't reveal—a collection of tents full of Manitobans who went to the track yesterday and who were among the few people that were hurting for him almost as much as he must have been hurting for himself.

Since the athletes arrived here, he's scarcely been able to work out. As recently as two days before his race, the doctors were warning him he shouldn't try to run. But he ran. He did it—wincing, grimacing, moving to the outside lane to let runners that he in a healthy state could normally run into the ground lap him. But he was there. He was at the Olympics.

I haven't been able to reach him by phone today but kind of don't think he's listening now. My guess is he's out cheering on some of his track and field teammates. If he were listening, I would like to tell him how much I admire what he did yesterday and to ask him not to quit. The winner of this year's 10,000-metre will probably go under 28 minutes. And my own guess is, with his injury healed and with the kind of shape he's brought himself back to, Chris McCubbins will be doing that kind of time himself and fairly soon. I hope he does. He deserves it.

When he received the *Morningside* tape, Chris couldn't listen to it. The race was just such a bad dream; he needed more time to recover. Sheldon Reynolds described it and why it was such a disappointment for Chris. Undoubtedly, the damage to his psyche took longer to heal than the damage to his body.

Chris went to the '76 Montreal Olympics in the best shape of his life, and he knew it but he was hurt. His groin was in rough shape, and after all the work the therapists could do, he managed to run the first mile and one-half with the leaders in his 10,000-metre heat, but then the groin went and Chris would not drop out. He finished last in his heat 32 min.+ and although physically it took a few months to heal, he took most of 1977 to recover psychologically from the devastation of not meeting his goals of placing well in the Olympic Games. It was a very tough time for Chris. Everyone could understand his disappointment but no one truly knew his deep sense of personal failure. We thought he was amazing to finish. Chris wasn't at the Games to just finish! He was very hard on himself, as usual!

Post Olympics

AFTER THE '76 GAMES, IT TOOK NEARLY A YEAR FOR CHRIS TO GET HIS body back in shape and to get his mind back around running. But, as the following story attests, real bandits beware.

In late May, 1977, Chris was laid up with another leg injury. He tried jogging but was too sore to continue. The next day he biked to school. He locked up the bicycle and went in to teach for the day. As he was coming out, he noticed a young guy fiddling with his bicycle—trying to remove some of the better parts. Chris yelled at him to stop. The thief had some interesting bits in his hand, so he decided to dash off with what he had. Perhaps if he'd known something about the attributes of the bike owner he might have just dropped everything and walked away. The culprit was going to be chased by an experienced racer. As Chris said, "The kid thought he was fast, but I knew I could catch him." Imagine the shock of the young thief when he realized he was going to be chased down and caught. What bad luck—stealing from a guy that competed last year in the Olympics. It was a short chase. In the entry of his running diary, it appeared that Chris was more pleased with how his leg felt than with catching the thief.

"Chased kid 400 m for ripping off stuff from my bike—leg felt fine."

Chris was putting more work into his academic qualifications. He was enrolled in the Bachelor of Education Program at the University of Manitoba and discovered a creative course in early childhood education offered at the University of California. In the spring and early summer of 1977, he attained a credit in Sensory Integration and Learning

Disorders: Screening and Training Children. The course credit was then transferred in 1978 to the University of Manitoba for credit toward year five in the Education program.

He was also back on the cross country running trails. Chris started competing again in October, 1977 and came in first at 22:43 in a 4.8-mile cross country meet in Brandon, Manitoba. He followed that with a win in the Prairie 12,000-metre Cross Country Championships in Saskatoon, Saskatchewan with a time of 38:51—even though he wrote *"felt a bit dead—had a stitch."* He kept up the momentum and won at the November 12 Canadian Cross Country Championship in Hull, Quebec. There were 118 runners and it was a tight, competitive race at the end. His running diary entry: *"Felt physically easy—course very muddy, rocky and dangerous."*

According to fellow runner Grant Towns, Chris thrived on these dangerous tracks.

> The tougher the cross-country course, the better Chris would run. One example is Halifax. Gravel and stones were embedded in the track. The trail was only two- feet wide in many spots. There was no place to pass. But Chris ate up these kinds of conditions. Here's another mental toughness issue. Fellow competitors would grumble about that kind of track—how can I run on this? Chris would accept it as another challenge. It also fit well with his no excuses for bad runs philosophy. It's similar with other conditions where you don't have any control. Poor footing—snow—sleet—rain are all in this category. A lot of runners will defeat themselves before they show up. You look outside—"do I really want to run in this today"' Chris' answer—"Yes, I run every day, irrespective of the conditions. This is a fun thing to do."

As a result of the Hull cross-country win, Chris was selected for the Canadian Cross Country team that would compete in Scotland in March, 1978. He was granted leave by the Winnipeg School Division to attend the games but was injured in the race. He placed 146th of 159 participants but, as was his custom, he finished the race.

Chris' dog Frodo was still running with Chris in 1978 and gaining further press coverage (October 10/78, *Winnipeg Free Press*, "Dogged Effort Pays Off"). Frodo started in a 10-km cross country race at Birds Hill Park with Chris in October of 1978 but ran only the first 2,000 metres. Then the tired dog sat out the remainder of the race waiting for her master to finish. The master came home a winner at 40:56.

CHRIS WAS STILL ENJOYING WORK AT KENT ROAD SCHOOL AND THE school was appreciative of his contributions. His principal, J. Hamm, provided the following good words as of April 13, 1978 in his teacher evaluation report.

> Mr. McCubbins is a very good teacher. He is friendly, co-operative, enthusiastic, reliable and hard-working. He has spent a lot of time planning, organizing and supervising an excellent physical educa-tion program for all primary pupils and teachers at the school. Mr. McCubbins is an asset to the Kent Road School.

As of September,1978, Chris decided to cut his teaching load in half—continuing at Kent Road School as the Kindergarten to Grade Six physical education teacher, but spending the freed-up hours at the University of Manitoba to attain his Education degree. Through the fall of 1978 and spring of 1979, Chris also supervised the U of M's track and field program. After a 10-km race, Chris was interviewed by the *Winnipeg Free Press* and provided some insights into why he was feeling ill.

> "My schedule is so full," he explained, "I teach phys-ed in the mornings, I'm coaching the Bisons [University of Manitoba cross country team] and also taking four courses towards my B. Ed. Degree, and I guess my resistance just broke down, and the flu just caught up with me."

On April 30, 1979, the Manitoba Track & Field Association published the five events in which Chris set a Manitoban record.

- A native record for the 1500-metre of 3:50.0 set in Winnipeg July 29, 1975.
- A native and open record for the 3000-metre of 8:09.2 set in Sudbury August 26, 1975.
- A native and open record in the 5000-metre of 13:44.8 set in Knoxville, May 8, 1976.
- A native & open record in the 10,000-metre of 28:16.6 set in Montreal, July 25, 1975.
- An open record (as an American) in the 3000-metre steeplechase of 8:38.2 set in Winnipeg July 30, 1967.
- A native record (as a Canadian) in the 3000-metre steeplechase of 8:40.8 set in Seattle June 17, 1972.

Many of these records were subsequently broken but not shattered. As of early 2013, the 28:16.6 record in the 10-km was the only one remaining. Sheldon Reynolds made the following observation.

Chris's only record left is the 10,000-metre, 28:16.6 on July 25/ 1976 in Montreal. His 3000- metre steeple record was broken only by two seconds by Henry Klassen; his 5,000-metre record by eight seconds by Chris Webber; and his 3,000-metre record by 13 seconds by Chris Webber. Most of them were broken in the 1990's—about 15 years after Chris set his times!

I would say with the results lately that Chris's 10,000-metre time will never be broken! Manitoba runners have rarely broken 30 minutes in the last two decades and it will take an African moving to Manitoba to do it! The 2012 London Olympic standard is 28:05.00, just 11.6 seconds better than Chris' time...37 years after he ran in Montreal in the pre-Olympic meet! Awesome time! The Mercier Tables compare event times and Chris' time is worth 891 points or equivalent to a 3:55.7 mile! Seeing as no one in Manitoba has ever run a sub four-minute mile.

At the London 2012 Olympic Games, Somali-born Mohamed Farah—now a British citizen—won the gold medal for the UK in the 10,000-metre race with a time of 27:30.42.

In the mid-seventies, Chris bought a home on Greenwood Place in Winnipeg's West End. Several of the Yellow Snow track members—Bruce Soulsby, Jim Lowe and Grant Towns—moved in and rented space. The neighbours might have thought that a bunch of other guys—Chris' close friends and members of the Yellow Snow track club—were also living there. They met at the Greenwood house to start their training runs and afterwards would stay over for a while to debrief, and time permitting, stay over longer for food and fun. Of course, on Sundays, Chris would cook up a breakfast of his famous whole wheat pancakes and if in season there would be blueberries. As many a Yellow Snow runner attested, "They were undoubtedly good for you but they seemed to just layer in your stomach. They just stuck there."

But the comfy boys club of Greenwood Place was about to end. Chris was scheduled to attend a running symposium that would change the course of his life. Lucky Chris!

Sue Jacobsen

AS A PHYSIOTHERAPIST, I WAS ASKED TO BE ON A COMMITTEE. IT WAS titled the Running and Related Injury Committee. Chris' roommate, Jim Lowe, was also on the committee. The committee organized a running symposium and Jim asked Chris to come. It was held on a Saturday evening in late January 1980.

There was a relay race and then a wine and cheese party. I ran the 800-metre and my brother ran 400. I had to do the race a second time—and was quite tired. After the race, Chris came over and complimented me on my running. My brother claimed he introduced us but I'm sure it was Jim Lowe.

My first impression was that Chris looked a bit seedy, with dark circles under his eyes, a straggly beard and long, seemingly unkempt hair curling into ringlets past his ears. But he had an aura that spoke far louder than his appearance—an aura of gentleness. I was drawn to this spirit as I was to his voice and his large, blue eyes.

Chris was so calm—there were just great vibes from the start. I was so taken by his eyes and that voice and his whole manner. I was in the middle of my physiotherapy exams so couldn't get together with him for coaching—but he mentioned a social to be held at one of the track clubs so I went with a girlfriend. I think it was a social to raise money for the Yellow Snow Track club.

What a great time. We danced the night away and had so much fun together. It was Feb 2, 1980. Then he invited me to a swim meet at Sargent Park Pool and afterwards we went to Casa Grande, the pizza place on the corner of Wall Street and Sargent. That was when I realized how much he could eat. He slowly and methodically ate the whole pizza. I had one piece. I had never seen anyone eat so much and yet—he stayed so trim.

We also went to a concert. One of the ladies at Concordia was involved in a musical production. I still remember the Fats Waller tune "Your Feet's too Big." Afterwards a work colleague remarked on how Chris was watching me. She said he was entranced. It's true we were so in love.

Then, we started running together that spring. I ran in high school but we started doing longer runs together. Then Chris asked me to move in with him on Greenwood since we were seeing each other so regularly. That spring I finished my bachelor's degree in physiotherapy.

There was an immediate attraction between us. We were in love. We were so tolerant of each other—but of course Chris was so tolerant of everyone. We both became stronger from the relationship.

Sue and Chris

SUE UNDOUBTEDLY WAS SURPRISED AT HOW WELL CHRIS COULD SWIM when he invited her to the Cardinal Swim Club meet at Sargent Park Pool. Chris probably hadn't yet talked about his time as an American pentathlete with either Sue or his colleagues in the club. Swimming wasn't his sport but he had a natural flair for it and during his time in the modern pentathlon improved immensely. It's no wonder at this Cardinal meet that he came first in the 200-metre freestyle in his 30-34 age group and second place overall with his time of 2:53.70. He was some 12 seconds off the overall winning time. Similarly, Chris was also first in his class in the 100-metre backstroke and third place overall in this event.

In May, 1980, both Sue and Chris entered the 10-km Run for Fun sponsored by the *Winnipeg Tribune*. Chris came in first with a time of 30:06 which was 53 seconds better than the 1979 result. The boys from Greenwood Place and their Yellow Snow running mates—Bob Walker, Bruce Soulsby, Greg Gemmell—also ran well. Sue finished at 39:12— second in her age class for females.

The *Winnipeg Tribune* estimated that there were 3,600 men, women and children who completed the 10-kilometre course, 2,662 of them officially registered. Registered entrants and hundreds of others swarmed at the starting line in front of the Assiniboine Park pavilion when park superintendent Wally Remple fired the starting pistol. Chris was asked how he found the race. Plagued by injuries in the past few years, he had been entering meets for the sheer joy of running.

> This is my third race in the last two years. I run 70 to 90 miles a
> week, which is half to two-thirds my normal training. I'm taking a

more enjoyable attitude to the sport. I'm not worrying about high-level competition anymore.

Undoubtedly, Chris was too busy in his new relationship to keep a running diary in 1980, but that is not the case in 1981. A revived and happy runner shines through. Every day there is an entry and every day there is a workout. He's running, swimming, cross-country skiing and cycling to work, lifting weights, and in the summer hiking and canoeing. There is a renewal that you can feel on the pages of his running journal—running a total of 6,209 kilometres and swimming 83,490 metres for the year.

In the next few months, Chris was running well, placing first in a series of races: a 15-km race at 46:13 on April 12; a 5-km race on April 26 at 14:29; an eight-km race on May 10 at 23:55; in the 10,000-metre Athletes Wear, Run for Fun on May 24 with a course record of 29:46 and then at the Charleswood In Motion 10-km on June 7 at 30:35.

He was back to Gimli on the August 2 long weekend to run in the Gimli 10-mile road race. Chris was first at 48:55 and Greg Gemmell was second at 50:45. Chris' comment in the diary was *"felt easy and relaxed."* Is this not the story of 1981?

This was the cold and rainy run where Chris turned to Greg and said 'C'mon let's go!' He needed someone to push him and that's just what Greg did. In training it was common for that to happen. Chris would train hard—often without a break—for the whole session. It was difficult to keep up with him, so his partners in running would take turns pushing him. Grant Towns explained.

> Chris thrived on hard workouts. There was virtually no rest—a very short 30 second break perhaps between intervals—but he would keep moving. We would train at La Barriere Park and Chris would go full out for the whole workout.
>
> We took turns pushing him. It wasn't an organized thing but it appeared to happen naturally. I would push him for one interval and then Sheldon might push him for the next. Then Karl would stay with him and run hard for a race. It seemed to work.

Chris finished the summer races at the end of August at Birds Hill Park participating in the Labatt's 20-km run. It was a close race where Jerry Kooymans of Toronto won with a time of 61:52. Kooymans said that his strategy was to hang back in the lead pack for a while to achieve a comfortable pace but that wasn't possible. Chris was right on his shoulder, so the strategy changed—he had to break away a little earlier. Typical Chris, his great stamina allowed him to push you in the middle of the race. David Edge, a British runner living at that time in Etobicoke, beat Chris in a sprint to the finish for second place at 62:21. Chris was third at 62:42. Chris' right groin tightened up and he had to stop partway through the race to stretch it. He was running for fun in the kind of tight race that he loved, but he still had that competitive zeal. He loved to win.

Even during fun-run training sessions with the Yellow Snow members, Chris was always ready for a race. Sheldon Reynolds put it this way.

> Chris was a phenomenal role model and mentor and he showed you how to plan to get better—and the work that had to go into the process. He had great psychological strength. But people who thought that when you went out for a run with Chris there was no sense of competition didn't know Chris. He loved competition, whether it was at cards or running or eating. It was O.K. as long as you were running a decent distance behind him, but as soon as you got close— say within 6 inches—it was game on and you had to respect that.

It must have been a cold January in 1982, for Chris had lots of diary entries about the weather. He began the year with the Manitoba Masters Swimming Championships. He was first in the 200-metre freestyle at 2:48.88, first in 100-metre backstroke at 1:17.53 and first in 200-metre backstroke at 3:22.08. Typical Chris, his diary lists the events and times but doesn't mention that he was first in each of the events. The ribbons were tucked away in his memorabilia.

Chris travelled to Victoria for the Victoria Cross Country Trials on February 7, 1982. He didn't finish the race. There seemed to be a combination of a stitch in his side and some sliding in his shoes. His comment: *"What's the point! Felt pretty discouraged, beautiful weather +10C."*

PERHAPS THIS OCCASION WAS ENOUGH TO GET CHRIS THINKING ABOUT the difference between the February weather in Victoria and that in Winnipeg—to get him thinking of the possibilities of a move to British Columbia. His diary comment on his return to Winnipeg confirms the theory:*"back to -22C, Bluck!"*

At the end of the 1981-82 school year, Chris was looking for a new teaching challenge. An opportunity arose at Winnipeg's Lord Roberts Community School. There was a unique and innovative program integrating nursery (pre-Kindergarten), Kindergarten and fourteen physically and mentally challenged students.

In this setting, Chris applied both his skills as a teacher and as an athlete. He was part of a four-teacher team working not only with the students but also with aides, attendants, therapists and community volunteers.

In 1983, Sue and Chris decided to relocate to Victoria, British Columbia. They sold their Winnipeg home and began to make plans. Sue was offered a job in Victoria and moved there in early April.

To assist in his quest for future employment, Chris solicited a number of letters of recommendation from principals at Kent Road and Lord Roberts Schools. Ivan Biblow, the Principal at Lord Roberts had many kind words:

> Chris has had a positive and successful year in this setting and we regret that he has found it necessary to relocate outside of Winnipeg.

He recommended Chris as a strong candidate for a teaching position, "especially one which would involve working with children at the primary or early childhood level."

The highest commendation came from John A. Buchanan, the Principal who had hired Chris at Kent Road School in 1974. He said things that Chris' friends, relatives, fellow runners or teaching colleagues would all have said, but John A said them better. He described the Chris they knew and loved.

> When I was the principal of Kent Road School we took on staff Mr. Chris McCubbins as a primary teacher at a time when male

teachers for very young children were very rare indeed. The experiment proved to be one of the best things we ever did.

Chris' athletic prowess and friendly, open manner made him an instant hero to the children of the school. First impressions were only confirmed and strengthened as the years went by.

Chris McCubbins is a young man of exemplary character, unpretentious and unassuming, full of fun and energy, hard-working, conscientious, and completely trustworthy. His relations with pupils, parents, and other staff members were excellent at all times. He was always willing to assist in the general activities of the school and did not confine his efforts to his own grade or class nor to regular school hours.

Chris McCubbins is an outstanding teacher. He has the magic touch with children; he gets them learning and at the same time thoroughly enjoying their school experience.

My honest opinion is that any school authority that can add Chris McCubbins to its staff will never regret the decision.

Chris ran a number of races—for one, the Puma 5-km at St. Vital Park in late March, 1983. He placed first at 15:02 in a field of 176 competitors even though he wrote that he *"felt dead and had a stitch in his side."* He ran the Puma 10-km at 30:06 at Kildonan Park on April 10, coming in first, even though he woke up late and had car trouble en route to the race. He made it a complete sweep by winning the Puma 15-km race at Assiniboine Park at 45:43. His comments:

> First by a lot, Walker 2nd—wind really slowed me last loop—a bit tired from yesterday's swim, tempo felt easy enough.

His final Winnipeg race of the year happened on the Pan Am track, a 10-km race in which he came first at 30:02. Then shortly afterwards, once the school year ended, Chris drove to Victoria to join Sue. He was going to spend the year as a substitute teacher in the Victoria school system.

On February 4, 1984, Chris participated in the Canadian Cross Country Championships at Beacon Hill Park in Victoria. It was a 7.5-mile or 12,110-metre course and a tight race. Chris came fifth at 37:04.5 and was only some 43 seconds off the winning time. As a result of his placement—fourth as a Canadian—Chris qualified for a position on the Canadian team competing in the World Cross Country Championship in Meadowlands Park, New Jersey on March 25. He didn't run in this race but did enter the Bloomsday Run held in Spokane, Washington on May 31. This was a 12-km race and Chris was 19th overall with a time of 36:59. The good news is that he was first in the 35-39-age category.

In June, 1984, Chris ran in the Maski-Courons race at St-Gabriel-de-Brandon, Quebec. It was a 20-km run—a longer distance than his usual runs. He placed fourth at 1:04.28.2. The winner was Dave Edge at 1:03.16.0.

In mid 1984, Sue and Chris moved back to Winnipeg. He was keeping fit in anticipation of future Masters Class races. New and interesting running events were looming.

CHRIS, JUNE 10, 2009

Another day another change in what is happening. The blasts (young rapidly producing abnormal white cells) in my blood are rising quickly. They were up to 17 % today. In yesterdays discussion with Dr Kumar he said if the blast cells in my bone marrow are above 10% a stem cell transplant is fruitless. They usually will not do a transplant at over 5% but would be willing to take the risk because of my otherwise wellness.

Today Dr Kumar did another biopsy to check my blast cells. He said the results would probably be ready by tomorrow so we made an appointment for 3PM.

Tip, Rilla, Sue and I went for a walk at Kilcona to look at the trees. Tip had not been to see the trees before. There were a lot of trees growing strongly and easy to see since the weeds have not gotten up yet. I saw the trees that Greg organized getting planted. They are doing well and nicely placed.

When we arrived at home there was a message from Dr Kumar. I called him back and learned that the blast count in my marrow is 40%. I am totally out of remission and any attempt at a transplant would have an almost nil chance of success. He did offer us another hope. There is a drug, Lenalinomide, which they found two case studies for. The patients had exactly the same cytogenetics that I do and in the two cases the patients achieved remission. The doctors could not find any reports of unsuccessful cases. This does not mean there are not unsuccessful cases. They just may not have been reported. As this is our only real hope we have asked for this treatment if possible. Our current understanding is that the new treatment is taken orally and we will be able to stay at home during the month or two of treatment with regular visits to Cancer Care. We now have to wait to see if we can obtain the needed drug since it is not one that is currently used for any treatment in Manitoba. Tip is temporarily out of a Donor Dog job. If I achieve remission from the new drug then he will be called on at that time. We will be meeting tomorrow with Dr Kumar to learn more.

As you can imagine it has been a very emotional day for us. We are leaping into the frontier of medical science and placing our final hope on the science and art of our caretakers. This is a huge step of faith. It seems that through this whole thing every time we feel like we are getting ahead we get bad news and every time we get bad news a new hope arises. It seems that we are on a path we do not understand but it is a course we are destined to follow. Hope still lives. Our path is very windy and difficult at times. I have to stay at peace and believe it will have a good and kind way.

Tonight we have tried to relax and be positive. We have called our family to tell them what has happened. Sue has been continuing to teach Tip to play crib.

CHRIS' 2009 DIARY

But life went on. Chris was home—there was hope for the success of the new drug. Diary entries tell the story.

June 12 Sue made cookies
June 13 Stephen Riley over a bit after 10 am, walk and visit

June 15 Lots of dreams related to treatment

June 17 Took first 2 Lenalidomide pills @ 8:45 am

June 20 Started to organize old training logs

June 22 I began working on cherry protection (netting)

June 25 Pulled nails out of boards from basement

June 27 watched "After Sunset" mystery comedy

June 28 OK sleep but feel tired lots of dreams

June 29 Picked up some hamburger buns from Tall Grass Prairie

July 1 Working on reinforcing cherry cage and sewing netting for cherry tepee

July 4 Watched IAAF Golden League Meet

July 8 Crib, my worst game ever 50-60 points behind

IT'S LITTLE WONDER THAT CHRIS DIDN'T EXPERIENCE DELAY IN HIS RE-turn to employment with the Winnipeg School Division. His record of service was exemplary both in and out of the classroom. As many teachers do, Chris worked over lunch hours and after school hours coaching softball, basketball, soccer and cross country running. At Kent Road School, he also involved the teachers in a pre-school fitness program.

He saw the young, impressionable students as more than faces looking back at him. Each child was an individual with unique needs of learning. As such, Chris spent as much classroom time as possible one on one with students.

Perhaps more importantly, in addition to their developing learning skills, Chris wanted his young charges to have fun. He was looking for ways to integrate the class such that they could enjoy activities together—activities that were non-competitive and in which everyone would feel comfortable participating. He found one activity where this happened—folk dancing. He had an inherent love of dance so it was no hardship for him to attend workshops on the art. As a result, he organized folk dance programs and staged evening performances for parents. He also organized an elementary schools folk dance festival.

On July 6, 1984, prior to his return to Winnipeg from the one-year hiatus to Canada's west coast, Chris received notice from the Winnipeg School Division that he had been appointed to a half-time teaching position at Riverview School in the Kindergarten program. His colleague in the French immersion portion of the program, Iris Muirhead, joined him one year later.

> Chris was always so relaxed in his approach to teaching and to children. He was gentle and quiet with the kids and let them explore and find out things on their own. There were lots of activities with putting things together and Chris was never worried about kids hammering thumbs—he was just so laid back. At the same time, he had an inherent confidence and a desire to expand his own horizons. One year the school needed someone to teach English to the French Immersion students and Chris volunteered and did a great job—not only for Kindergarten kids but also for grades 1, 2 and 3.
>
> We shared the philosophy that young children should be involved in hands-on, fun activities rather than staged practised performances. One example was the Christmas concert. We organized a rhythm band for the Kindergarten participants—that way all the students could participate freely and without pressure.
>
> Sue and Chris and I were interested in understanding our personalities so partook of the Enneagram exercises. Unlike Sue and me, Chris would be best described as a rock in a stream—not easily moved. The water flowed around him. He surely never liked confrontation.
>
> He was also so ultra-modest about his athletic accomplishments. To this day I am not sure how many years I knew Chris before I learned what an exceptional athlete he really was. I was aware he biked or ran to school but had no idea of his many racing successes or that he was still competing at an elite Masters level. He certainly never drew attention to himself about his abilities.

Chris' relaxed but focused approach to teaching is reflected in an end-of-year letter from a parent. At the first Meet the Teacher night, Chris—in his off-handed way—suggested that he didn't know why anyone would have their children in his room when they could be in the French immersion class next door. The parent didn't take the remark as an off-hand comment and at first felt unsure about her decision. Then as the year progressed, because of her child's development, she became completely comfortable with Chris' approach. She wrote,

> He needed your type of program. I think you underestimated your-self and the value of what you were doing. Under your guidance the children have been learning to deal with situations on their own and to express themselves creatively in their own personal way. The con-fidence they build in themselves now will help them in later years.

Her child liked the ice cream treat that Chris gave them unexpectedly one afternoon "for no specific reason!" Chris' "let's have fun" approach to teaching was honed at an early age. One day back in Grade Six, at-tending Jefferson School in Enid, Chris carried in his pet lamb for the enjoyment of the first-grade students. The lamb and the students both had their photos in the local paper. The kids felt the soft wool and fed the lamb from a bottle and then wrote stories about the experience. Chris was celebrating spring and realized early on how to capture both the attention of early learners and also that of the local press.

Marie and Chris tenting at Lake Tahoe, early June 1968. *Photo courtesy of Heather Stafford.*

Chris, early 1969, doing basic US Army training at Ft. Polk. He ran a 4:46 mile in combat boots. *Photo courtesy of the McCubbins family.*

A July 1977 photo of the McCubbins and Chaney families. Back row from the left as related to Chris: brother Phillip, sister Rilla Chaney, brother-in-law Marvin Chaney, brother Tipton, Chris. Front row: niece Nathania Chaney, mother Juanita, father Clarence and niece Anne Chaney. *Photo courtesy of the McCubbins family.*

A group of Yellow Snow Track Club members at Labarriere Park, Winnipeg prior to a training session, Spring 1978. From left to right: Karl Sproll, Jim Feathers, Grant Towns, Greg Gemmell, Chris, Bruce Soulsby, Bob Moody, Gary Swanson, Sheldon Reynolds and Frodo the dog. *Photo courtesy of the Yellow Snow Track Club.*

Chris, canoeing in Manitoba. *Photo courtesy of Sue Jacobsen.*

Chris and Sue, 1987. *Photo courtesy of Sue Jacobsen.*

Frodo, Chris' long-time running companion and a dog in Olympic-class condition after 19 years of cross country running. *Photo courtesy of the McCubbins family.*

Sue and Chris running in Enid, Oklahoma. *Photo courtesy of Sue Jacobsen.*

Chris in 1999 at the banquet for his induction into the Manitoba Sports Hall of Fame. *Photo courtesy of Sue Jacobsen.*

Chris is instructing his young charges in the finer points of cross country skiing during a session at the 'Great Get Off Your Butt and Ski' Program, Windsor Park Trails, Winnipeg. *Photo courtesy of Sue Jacobsen.*

Tree planting memorial, September 2012, at Chris McCubbins Cross Country Trails, Kilcona Park, Winnipeg. Long time running mates from left to right: Karl Sproll, Sheldon Reynolds, Darren Klassen, Michael Booth, Greg Gemmell, Grant Towns. *Photo courtesy of the author.*

Sue at the tree planting memorial of September 2012, Chris McCubbins Cross Country Trails, Kilcona Park, Winnipeg. *Photo courtesy of the author.*

The Masters Runner

IN NOVEMBER, 1985, 40-YEAR-OLD CHRIS MCCUBBINS QUALIFIED AS A Masters Runner. He spent some time that fall of 1985 seeking running venues that included a Masters category. The next few years were productive ones for Chris; he was running some of his best races ever and winning prize money.

He started off the running year in good form, placing first in the 3000-metre Boeing Indoor Track Classic with a time of 8:24. Allan Besson of the *Winnipeg Free Press* described the race in a February article.

> In case the young lions who are the up and coming long distance runners in this province had thoughts of taking over as king of the hill, Chris McCubbins, who recently turned 40, set those thoughts aside at the recent Boeing Indoor track Classic.
>
> Running what he termed a slow race, McCubbins blew the field away in the open men's 3,000 metres, and looked stronger at the finish line than he did at the start.
>
> Humble in victory, McCubbins said, "It was quite a bit slower than my personal best. I think that there might have been too many people entered in it. They also started it late."
>
> It was a classic McCubbins victory. Starting well back in the field, McCubbins laid back for three laps before moving to the outside and shifting into high gear.
>
> The gold medal winner for the United States in the 3000-metre steeplechase at the 1967 Pan American Games in Winnipeg said he isn't trying any kind of a comeback as was suggested by one of the

railbirds watching the race. "I'm just trying to stay healthy and run fast. My personal best in 1975 was 8:09."

If he has a shortcoming, it's his history of injuries. "Health-wise I'm doing fine right now," he said. "I'm being pretty cautious."

In May, 1986, Chris and Sue joined another 511 runners in the annual Athletes Wear 10-km run. Chris was first overall at 30:39 and Sue had the best time for female runners at 37:53.

Chris was ranked as the top master runner in Canada and number four in the world by *Runner's World* magazine. Chris had run a 10,000-metre event at the University of Manitoba oval earlier in the week. He came in first at 30:27 and after the Athletes Wear race said he felt somewhat tired. Typically, he didn't blame it on the earlier run but indicated that he had to do more speed workouts to get back to a level of training typical of his past.

On June 29, 1986, Chris ran at the Cascade Run-Off in Portland, Oregon. It's a 15-km (9.3 miles) Road Race. There was an official description of the course that would appeal to the casual walker as well as runners.

> This year's course is identical to the Cascade run-off course used since 1983. The famous race course begins and ends in downtown Portland, with major portions covering beautiful scenic areas with breathtaking views. Beginning on the east end of the Burnside Bridge, the course heads west over the Willamette River, turns south onto Broadway through downtown Portland. From there, it's a gradual ascent along Terwilliger Parkway to Elk Point and then mostly gradual downhill, to a flat and fast finish along Barbur Boulevard and Front Avenue.

There was a class field of international runners with master runner Mike Hurd of England being touted as the man to beat. Chris was first in his 40-44 age class (Masters) at 46:06.75 and 25th overall. Hurd finished third behind Chris and Guenter Mielke of West Germany, who ran a 46:19.

The Cascade race officials recorded Chris' time as the third-best time ever in the 40-44 age class. Antonio Villanueva, who was 43 when running in the 1984 race, set the best time ever at 45:44. Villanueva also held the second-best time for the 40-44 age class in 1985 at 45:50.

On August 9, 1986 Chris ran in the Asbury Park 10-km Classic (6.21 miles). Asbury Park is a city in Monmouth County, New Jersey located on the Jersey Shore. It's part of the New York City Metropolitan area. The city has a population of around 16,000 and has gained notoriety for its association with singer Bruce Springsteen and for the fact that it was ranked the sixth-best beach in New Jersey in the 2008 Top 10 Beaches Contest sponsored by the New Jersey Marine Sciences Consortium.

Unfortunately, in October 2012, the city, its boardwalk and surroundings suffered great damage from Hurricane Sandy.

Chris was 31st overall at 30:49 but won $1000 for being first in the Masters Class; Mike Hurd from England was second in this class at 31:11 and received $500. The winning open time was 28:57. The *Asbury Park Press* of August 10, 1986 made the following observations about the race:

> Over 5200 were entered and at least 20 of them stayed together in the front pack for over two miles. Slowly, the contenders pulled away from the pretenders. Yet five were still duelling it out in the final sprint back to the Hall.
>
> Leading "older man" was 40-year-old Canadian star Chris McCubbins of Winnipeg, 31st overall and Masters 40-44 champion in 30:49.
>
> The internationalism of it all—Olympians of 12 countries were represented—moved right along as the rest of the giant pack dashed to the finish line.
>
> The race's biggest name of all—Henry Rono of Kenya, one-time holder of four world records—made a surprise return to big-time racing by placing 38th.

It was off to Portland, Oregon at the end of June, 1987 for his second run in the Cascade Run-Off 15-km (9.3 miles) Road Race. There were 7500 runners entered. Chris, at 41 years of age, was first in the Masters category and 22nd in the open at 45:34.84, the only Canadian in the top 25 runners.

In a letter dated on July 30, 1987, Charles A. Galford, president of Cascade Run Off, congratulates Chris.

> In repeating as Cascade Run Off Masters champion, you finished 22nd overall and set a new North American record with an amazing clocking of 45:34.84.

Chris beat Villanueva's old record by 9 seconds. This was also the first year that the Masters division offered prize money, so Chris picked up a purse of $1,000 for his efforts.

In addition to prize money for the masters, drug testing became a part of this year's race. The top three runners in the men's and women's divisions, plus two random selections from the top 25, were tested for anabolic steroids and various stimulants. President Chuck Galford indicated that runners, for the most part, were coming up clean. He knew of only one road runner who had tested positive, and that was at the 1986 New York City Marathon.

Chris was surely in the right company. He was an honest runner with the sole intent of getting better at his craft and beating his own times. He wasn't interested in taking drugs to improve his performance. It just wasn't in his make-up. You got better by working harder and longer—eating the right foods and living right. He and the Yellow Snow members were in this for the long term and adopted Chris' credo—"Eat right, Train Hard and Don't Cheat."

The Western Canada Game Trials were held on July 12, 1987. Chris finished second at 30:34.0 and running mate Grant Towns at 32:50.5. It was a good tune-up for Chris and Grant for their upcoming August 8 Asbury Park Classic Run.

At Asbury Park, there were some 5200 runners who moved forward at the sound of the 9:00 am starting gun. It was the largest racing field in the state, and despite the heat and high humidity, nearly all of them finished the race. Chris came in 24th overall and first in his Masters class at 30:57.

One week later, on Sunday, August 16, Chris was entered in the Falmouth Road Race in Cape Cod placing first in the Masters Class. Here's a quote from the *Cape Cod Times.*

> The Masters Race turned into a dual between Chris McCubbins of Winnipeg and Larry Olsen of Millis Mass. McCubbins won by 19 seconds, finishing 32nd overall in 34:34.
>
> McCubbins, 41, might have to contend with the likes of Bill Rodgers and Grant Shorter if he hopes to successfully defend next year. Shorter becomes a Master when he turns 40 in December. Both were on hand for a clinic Saturday night and said they're looking forward to racing again when they move into the new age group division.

Sue and Chris completed the 1987 American running circuit on August 22 at the 9th annual Maggie Valley Moonlight Race in North Carolina—an eight-km run. There were 1,347 male runners and Chris was 43rd overall and fifth in the Masters Class 40-49 age group. Sue was 28th of 570 female runners at 31:55. Sue wrote in her running diary that *"Chris had a virus—a bad one."*

It was little wonder that the Manitoba Runners' Association voted Chris as the Manitoba Runner of the Year in 1987. But early in 1988, he and Towns would receive additional accolades. They were listed by *Runner's World* magazine among the top 21 Masters Runners in the world. Chris was ranked sixth and Towns 21st. At the Cascade and Asbury Park runs of 1987, Chris finished first in his class ahead of the top three ranked runners—Mike Hurd of Great Britain, Antonio Villanueva of Mexico and Atlaw Belilgne of Ethiopia.

As a Masters runner, Chris was still running for the joy of running but he continued to compete in local races over the next several years—especially the Athletes Wear 10-km Run for Fun, the spring Puma series and Islendingadagurinn 10-mile road race from Winnipeg Beach to Gimli. His Yellow Snow compatriots continued to run with him.

In the 1988 Athletes Wear 10-km race, Chris was first at 31:02 and Greg Gemmell second at 31:57.

CHRIS CONTINUED TO KEEP A RUNNING DIARY. IN THE APRIL 1989 PUMA Series, Chris was third in the 15-km run. His diary entry read:

> Splits (5:05, 15:56, 32:52) legs died about 3K, shoulders knotted too, let off at 5K

At the 10-km June 4, 1989 Athletes Wear event at Assiniboine Park, Chris wrote *"fairly relaxed, controlled"* for his first place 31:02 run. The *Winnipeg Free Press* article described it this way:

> Veteran runner Chris McCubbins ran away from the field yesterday to win the Athlete's Wear 10-km Run for Fun at Assiniboine Park. McCubbins crossed the finish line in a time of 31 minutes and two seconds, 55 seconds ahead of runner-up Greg Gemmell.

On June 18, 1989 at the Cascade Run-Off, Portland's 15-km road race, Chris placed 41st overall and third at 46:43.90 in the Masters class. It was a competitive international array of runners. For example, there was 40-year-old Kenyan Wilson Waigwa, who came in first in the Masters class at 46:08.34. With the exception of two runners from the US, the first 25 placing runners were from outside North America. From Chris' running diary:

> 46:44, 4:45 mile, 16:00 5K, 31:45 10K—stomach seized up, left calf cramped some

Chris came back to Manitoba and again won the August 6, Icelandic Race, at 53:14. Sue was first among females at 66:28. Later in August, Chris ran the 20-km Birds Hill race and came first at 1:05.44. He recorded his split times at 5:10, 16:10, 32:30, and 49:07. Chris ended the outdoor season capturing the 10-km Manitoba Senior Cross Country Championships on October 7 at Maple Grove Park. There were 27 men and 13 women competitors. Just for a change, Chris ran in bare feet, posting a winning time of 32:03.

Chris the Coach

DARREN KLASSEN, A 23-YEAR-OLD COMPETITIVE 5000-METRE RUNNER, was looking for a coach in the late eighties. Bruce McKay, his current coach and fellow Yellow Snow club member, was moving out of province. Darren wondered if Chris would take on the task and he did. The Barcelona Olympics of 1992 were approaching and Darren wanted to be there. Chris had been to the Olympics and knew the rigours of that game.

> Chris was different from most other coaches I had encountered. He was completely laid back. His workout philosophy was "let's go and have some fun." He had so much internal drive and understood that he didn't need to be all over me. He never used too many words but when he spoke he meant it. There was a very kind way about him. If I ran poorly, I never had the sense that I'd let him down. The only time I heard his voice raised was in competition, booming across the track—"Go now! Go now!"

Undoubtedly, Chris had set up a program for Darren that was honed from Chris' own experiences plus his penchant for staying current with new coaching practices. He kept in touch with his tutor Jack Daniels but he went beyond that. He was able to set a program into which, Darren realized, he had put a huge amount of thought. Chris was continually researching, in large part to expand his own knowledge. He brought all his athletic, leadership and educational experiences to coaching.

> The workouts that Chris organized were punishing. The training regime consisted of two days of hard workouts followed by two days

of easy. The hard days were intense. Chris knew that the Olympic format—first the heats, and then the run-offs and finally one day of rest—meant that I would be running tired in the final and he needed to prepare me for that. Chris was always pushing me as an athlete but that's what attracted me to him. I knew that you didn't get there without hard work.

From his early days at OSU and then later with the University of Manitoba track club, Chris was always a proponent of running on grass. He knew that it preserved the body from the shock of pavement where the energy tends to bounce back at you through tender joints. Sometimes he would even have Darren run barefoot, another spin-off from Chris' early days of training.

Chris set up a unique set of exercises. He placed much emphasis on building up strength in the joints and muscles to prevent injury from the impact of jolts to the legs. Running on an uneven grass surface assists in that preparation. They would start from Chris' home and make their way over to Churchill Drive, a grassy, peaceful riverside stretch of Winnipeg popular with many joggers and runners. Afterwards, they often returned to Chris' home for pancakes.

They were the healthiest pancakes you could eat. Of course, Sue and Chris loved to garden so he would throw in all these great ingredients. The pancakes didn't look that great—green from all that garden goodness—but they were undoubtedly full of nutrients."

Darren was also amazed at what Chris could eat. He called him an "unbelievable eater." Darren figured he could hold his own with most appetites but Chris was exceptional. He wasn't the first to come to that conclusion.

The summer of 1991 was the last in which Darren ran competitively. He was feeling tired and run down and after a battery of tests, his doctor referred him to Minnesota's Mayo Clinic. He was young and fit but all of a sudden he had no energy. The diagnosis was chronic fatigue syndrome. The process of recovery was long and competitive running was not part of it.

I had lived to compete at the 1992 Games and hoped to make the standard in 1991. Chris was very supportive thru those tough times. I tried to distance myself from the community of runners. I was just so devastated by not being able to run competitively and train and achieve the goals that I had set. So, I went from seeing Chris some 3 times per week to nothing. The Olympic dream was dead.

Three years later, I got my head around the situation. It was Chris' philosophy. You run because you love running and that was me. I was feeling better, I missed running and I wanted to get back in shape so I started running again. And typically with Chris, the door was always open to come back and get back into the training routine.

Darren Klassen was able to capture the essence of Chris McCubbins— his character, his attitude and philosophy of life and his experiences of running and coaching—in a meaningful way.

Chris' coaching was an extension of his own running. The way to achieve success was through hard work, perseverance and a positive attitude. He coached in the same way as he ran. Chris never got too excited about successes and also never got down with failures. He always was thinking to the future and not to the past. He showed how to treat setbacks as lessons and not obstacles. There was always another opportunity around the corner. Chris modelled what he taught. He helped me and those around him to believe in themselves—that a person could ask no more of themselves than to do their best. These characteristics were not only keys to athletic success but also life success.

Sue Recalls the 1990 Travel Adventure

IN OCTOBER OF 1990, WE SET OFF ON ANOTHER GREAT ADVENTURE. Both Chris and I took leaves of absence and travelled for much of the year. The trip began with us driving west to Creston, BC for my youngest brother Jim's wedding. We then visited family and friends in BC before driving south to San Anselmo, California, where we stayed with Chris' sister Rilla and her family.

From there we flew to Hong Kong—in late October early November of 1990 and spent ten days around the city. Then we made a five-day trip into China—very interesting. We tried to find swimming pools wherever we travelled so that we could get some exercise. We did a lot of touristy things—enjoyed walking and eating and always had cooked things so we didn't get sick. Then from Hong Kong we flew to Thailand—landed in Bangkok, the capital and took a taxi to the outskirts of the city. We were horrified by the noise and the pollution so took an air-conditioned bus south down the coast and spent Christmas day on the beach in Thailand.

We went through Malaysia—travelled with locals—hanging out the side of the bus—carrying our huge backpacks. We were tired and I remember waiting three hours for a bus in Indonesia. We couldn't read the writing. Then to Singapore. It was such a clean city. We became accustomed to eating lots of vegetarian food. We took a flight to Bali—travelled on the cheap—and from there to Gili Air a small island in Indonesia. There were minimum comforts. We tried snorkelling but decided not to dive.

From there we went to Australia—to Perth. Lots of people on the trip to China were either Australians or New Zealanders. We often stayed with folk we met. We belonged to an organization called SERVAS. There are interviews to establish your acceptance to the organization and rules when you call a host. For example, you can only stay two nights. The host must share some time with you— describe spots of interest or the geography or the culture. Usually, the host shares a meal with you and this is a great opportunity to exchange information. We had a particularly fabulous time staying with SERVAS people in Australia and New Zealand. Those people were so friendly. When we travelled south from Perth the host gave us his car—an older model. He was appreciative that Chris was able to fix the side window for him. They also invited us on a three-day canoe trip which we loved. We were used to going on camping trips very Spartan-like—cheese and crackers and powdered rations—just what you could carry on your back. But this is not the way Aussies go canoeing—they fill their eskies—their ice coolers—with gourmet meals. They carry lots of beer and wine and clothes and they are so generous in sharing. We did the 36-hour bus trip from Perth to Adelaide, slept on the bus and fell into a mindset where we took each day as it came.

It was funny—Chris became much more social. He became more talkative and much more aware of how fortunate we were and how well off we were relative to others. As a result, we became cognizant of the need to assist others who were less fortunate than us.

Chris and I were away for about eight months. When we returned home we began donating to Plan International as a small way to help in poorer countries. We also began hosting SERVAS guests from many countries. They would stay with us for one or two days as they travelled on their great adventures as Chris and I had done on ours. Of course, the trip also expanded our cooking repertoire to curries from Malaysia and Thailand and we enjoyed inviting friends over to experience these foods.

I returned to the same job and Chris joined the staff at David Livingstone School.

Back in the Classroom

CHRIS WAS THE BEST PERSON TO MEET THE CHALLENGES OF TEACHING at David Livingstone School—an inner-city nursery to Grade 8 Winnipeg school. His students, their parents and his fellow teachers were the beneficiaries.

We know how at home Chris was on a cross-country trail or steeple-chase course or track. He was equally at home in a classroom with his gift of patience and empathy for young learners. Chris was well suited to early childhood education.

Perhaps his early summer work at camp after his freshman college year or his role in managing a summer program for children at Gimli in the early seventies were contributing factors. Something sparked his interest.

There were a number of key factors that made him a successful teacher and role model to students. Fellow teachers provided the details. Chris had great empathy for his students—he genuinely felt for the kids, especially for those who were impoverished. As a result, Chris had wonderful rapport with the children and they gave him the ultimate respect.

At David Livingstone School, Chris had a dual role as a full-time teacher. Half his time was spent as an instructor introducing his kids to the world of computers and the other half was spent as an early childhood educator. While sister Rilla was visiting Chris and Sue, Chris invited her to join him in the David Livingstone classroom.

I was amazed that he knew each parent's name. Chris would greet them at the door, shake their hand and usher their child into the classroom. I noticed, after a whole day in the class, he never raised his voice. He devoted several minutes of private time with each child—encouraging them in their learning.

When the Grade 5 class was ready for computer training, they were eager to go. They left their home class and filed in to Chris' computer lab taking seats at stations assembled in a U shape around the walls. There was method to his design. The configuration allowed for an empty space in the middle of the room—adequately removed from the stations. There were seldom problems of discipline, for Chris had earned the respect of his students. But, if there was misbehaviour and a need for order, Chris would sit the rascal facing a back wall of nothingness. Five minutes would suffice.

Chris was a valuable asset in the classroom. He was a terrific male role model for the early childhood pupils. He had learned the skills of computing on his own and was able to teach others. In addition, he had all the attributes of his athleticism and passed on his passion for fitness to both fellow students and teachers.

Chris maintained a high level of fitness throughout his life, as verified by former coach Jack Daniels.

Jack Daniels Retests for Fitness

IN THE MID NINETIES, COACH JACK DANIELS GATHERED TOGETHER HIS 26 Alamosa runners and re-tested them for fitness. As previously stated, the typical runner lost about 1 unit of fitness value each year, beyond the age of 40, so at age 50, a 78.6 value would be down to about 53 ml/kg. But here was an exceptional case, as Daniels explains.

Not Chris. When I re-tested all 26 of my research subjects, 25 years after those initial tests back in 1968, the average max value was in the mid-50s, as might be expected. However, Chris' VO2max at age 50 was 76 ml/kg. To my knowledge no 50-year-old has ever had that high of a VO2max. Of all the other great runners in that study, including some who had been in the 80s for VO2max when they were in their 20s, only two others were over 70 and they were just a little over 70. That doesn't happen if you don't stay in shape, and Chris was the greatest at doing just that.

A really great thing I learned from Chris as a result of that follow-up study was the importance of taking time off when injured or sick. He had documented every day that he did not train due to injury or illness for that 25-year period, and days off totalled over 1200. Now if you figure that out, it is only about 48 days off each year (less than once each week), but every time Chris was sick or had a little injury he rested himself and without doubt he was the fittest human ever for age 50. I always refer to this finding when I deal with runners I coach, and try to impress upon them the importance of resting when hurt or injured.

There was no doubt that Chris kept fit throughout his life. Exercise was a part of his being. But taking time off from injury was a stretch. Chris' running diary proves contrary. He didn't like idle time, often jumping back into training when rest would have been the better course. His good friend and running mate Sheldon Reynolds agreed.

> Chris had a bad track record on this front. He had the philosophy that the guy competing next to him was working hard when he was injured and doing nothing. Now, that competitor had that much more of an advantage on him so he couldn't really afford the luxury of slacking off. He had to keep pushing—and this is what Chris did. This was especially evident in the lead-up to the 1976 Olympic run. He needed a month of healing not a month of running.

One More Run

PHYSICALLY AND PSYCHOLOGICALLY, CHRIS HAD COME A LONG WAY IN his fight with leukemia—a long, hard struggle—even though by August of 2009 it was only 6 months from initial diagnosis and treatment. As Chris remarked, after previous falls he was always able to bounce back, but this was a more troublesome foe.

Throughout his illness, he kept his friends and family in touch by e-mail.

NOW, CHRIS TELLS US THE BALANCE OF HIS STORY—EVER THE OUTLIER, the coach and the architect of dreams.

CHRIS, AUGUST 7/09

Another 7-hour day at Cancer Care. We just got home about 7:45. I received the antibiotics and packed blood cells (Hemoglobin). My temperature remained within the normal range today, indicating that the antibiotic is helping. Tomorrow we go back at 10:30 AM so they have time to do blood tests and can get the results back by the time I finish my antibiotic.

We did get out for a short walk this morning before light rain started and after breakfast Sue practiced the Touch of Healing she has been learning.

Hopefully tomorrow will be a shorter day and we will have more time and energy to communicate.

SUE, AUGUST 8/09

As often happens when people walk close to death and dying, we have become more open to our spiritual selves. We have both been touched by and have grown towards God, who I know is walking with us on this difficult journey. We have both seen the strength of our bond and our fervent hope is that God has future plans for both of us as a couple.

The Outlier

CHRIS DIDN'T READ MANY BOOKS BUT WHILE IN HOSPITAL FIGHTING his battle with leukemia, he read *The Outliers: The Story of Success* by Malcolm Gladwell. It was a book that he couldn't put down and enjoyed discussing with everyone who would listen—especially his sister Rilla. The book resonated with Chris because of its theories and examples as to how people become proficient and successful in what they do, whether it's Bill Gates as a successful entrepreneur, Yo-Yo Ma as a successful cellist or Wayne Gretzky as a successful hockey player. They are people whose achievement falls outside of normal experience.

The date of your birth and the cut-off date for schooling are important. For example, there is an advantage if you are the oldest child in the class and you are also a talented athlete. Because of your age and the speed of child development, you are likely to be more physically mature. You will be chosen for teams and get a chance to play and thus have an opportunity to get better—an advantage over your younger cohorts.

Chris could relate to this phenomenon. He happened to be the youngest in the class and in tenth grade was only some five feet tall—a skinny little guy who didn't get picked for sports teams. He had to find his own sports niche—with his brother's help. By Grade 12 he was six feet two inches tall and had proven himself as a runner. But he was still at a disadvantage as a freshman runner at OSU. He was surely competitive in the mile and two-mile races but hadn't reached his peak since he was relatively younger than the other athletes. As fellow runner Jim Metcalf pointed out, if Chris' freshman year had been delayed, he would have had many more accolades and undoubtedly would have broken a number of college records.

Timing as to when you enter an activity is important. Bill Gates was on the cusp of a technological revolution—he had the good fortune to be there on the first swell of the movement and time to get loads of experience in his field. Gladwell mentions a figure of 10,000 hours to become sufficiently proficient in something. Chris too felt that he got into the sport of running at an opportune time. He was on the cusp of a revolution in the science of running—studying the physiology of the runner and what the runner had to do to get better. He met Jack Daniels, who was devoting his life's work to this quest and was tested by Jack early on. Chris used the results to get better. The sport was drug free on Chris' entry and Chris remained an honest, drug-free participant. He adopted a personal philosophy of seeking the best practices for improvement whether those practices were diet, running routines or weight training. Because he started when he did—in Grade 10—it wasn't hard for Chris to put in the 10,000 hours fairly early in his career. Thus, when he got to a starting line he didn't have to think about how he was going to run—the technique was already engrained in his psyche.

Gladwell has a chapter titled "Trouble with Genius." The gist is that someone can have lots of talent but no support system to see him through. There are many reasons why this might happen. Some cultures are disadvantaged in terms of their access to books or schooling opportunities. Or perhaps there is a person with great talent and a desire to pursue that talent at the university level but there is no money for funding. Or someone has talent but they get misdirected by drugs or alcohol or gangs or some other inhibitor. Someone has to come to the rescue—understand the person and the talent—see the lost opportunity if this person is not supported and do the right thing. Undoubtedly, Chris must have been grateful for the support he received. How many times did Sue use her patience and physiotherapy skills to keep Chris running? But on the other side, Chris was also a true enabler—a person that recognized the call and did something about it. He proved it in his coaching of others and in his nurturing of children.

At David Livingstone School, Chris saw the encumbrances that his students faced. They didn't come from homes with lots of books or computers or athletic equipment. They were missing many of the advantages of their more affluent neighbours in other parts of the city. Chris saw that it was his responsibility to make amends for such geographical and income inequality. At first his classroom didn't have computers so he scrounged and begged and borrowed until he had what he wanted. It wasn't exactly what he wanted in some cases because he had to settle often for hardware that others didn't want. Nevertheless, he brought these kids some sense of equality of opportunity. Chris did the same thing in the "Get Off Your Butt" cross country ski program and for the planning and development of Kilcona Park. He saw the need and took action.

CHRIS, AUGUST 6

Today is the first day I can remember in a long time not having a Central Line, PICC, or hep-lock sticking out of my body for putting something into it or taking blood out of it. I will probably have something back in by tomorrow, so I am enjoying the feeling.

The steroid cream I have been using on my face is helping a great deal. I am not nearly as bright red or tingly. We can actually see a little normal skin on my cheeks. It is interesting that my nose has not gotten the rash and only a few little spots above and below my lips. I had a pretty good night sleep especially for being in the hospital, not a place to go for rest, but a good place for care. My infection appears to be under control for now and hopefully the antibiotic will finish it off.

This morning I had just begun breakfast (breakfast tends to be late on GD6) when the nurse came in to prepare me for my bone marrow aspiration. The difference between a biopsy and an aspiration is they only take fluid from the bone (for an aspiration) but none of the actual bone. An aspiration is therefore easier to recover from. Ewoma, one of the RCAs (Registered Clinical Assistants) are members of the team from other countries that for some reason do not qualify as doctors here, did my aspiration today. Ewoma is a wonderful quiet spoken lady from Nigeria. She did an excellent job with me only feeling the slightest pain a few times as she did the deadening. It has been several hours now since the aspiration and I am having no problems with the area.

We basically learned nothing new today.

I just received a call from Dr Kumar's receptionist that I will be meeting with him on Wednesday instead of Tuesday. Some of the information we will need for making an informed decision may not even be ready by then. The good side is we do not have to go to Cancer Care tomorrow. A day off and an extra day with nothing sticking out of my body. The extra day will also give us a chance to recover from the stress of the last few days. I am feeling much better than on Saturday when I went onto D6 but am still tired. I will try to get out some but have to be careful as the sun and heat seem to increase the intensity of the rash.

The team at Cancer Care and D6 continue to work doing their best for us. It is amazing the hours and energy they put in on a daily basis to help the patients under their care. We have grown to appreciate their dedication and caring attitude. It helps us to remain positive.

We continue to rely and thrive on each other's support. At times the emails and cards we receive bring tears as we realize how fortunate we are to have so many wonderful people supporting us.

Your support and prayers have been very important in helping us keep our spirits up.

Tomorrow is the beginning of a very important two days of decision making. In the morning I will have my 7th (hopefully lucky 7). Then on Tuesday we will meet with Dr Kumar to discuss the results. Those results will determine in which direction our treatment will go. Although our fatigue levels are increasing, our inner spirit is growing.

CHRIS, AUGUST 12/09

Today's news is the news we never wanted to hear. Dr Kumar spent over an hour with us today. There are no more treatments left that can be used to cure me. I am being shifted into the Palliative program.

Dr Kumar also talked to us about end of life and that the type of leukemia I have is usually not associated with pain.

I wish we had better news. It has been a very difficult day telling our family.

We will be refocused soon and raising our spirits to enjoy the rest of my life as much as we can.

Get Off Your Butt and Ski

FOR SOMEONE WHO COULD BARELY STAND ON CROSS COUNTRY SKIS when he first tried them, Chris later became a high-level competitive cross country skier. The first time he went out, he couldn't maintain his balance. He was falling continuously—a laughing matter to his Yellow Snow compatriots. Not so many years later, he was not only skiing classically but was skate skiing and competing in the sport. Chris had the last laugh.

As a result of his love for the outdoors, he had a dream of getting kids involved—especially the kids that he taught, youngsters that would normally not have the opportunity to ski. Their families didn't have the money to buy skis, poles and boots and if they did, where would they ski? Chris took on the challenge. He planned and implemented a course of action. As a result, Chris secured equipment, shuttled students to the ski trails and taught them how to ski. Here was the genesis of The Great Get Off Your Butt and Ski Program.

On his own time, Chris gathered ski equipment. He scoured garage sales, badgered friends, commandeered the time and resources of his Yellow Snow teammates and in the process, gradually assembled suitable equipment. Later he coerced the corporate community to back his cause. He sold the concept to his students at David Livingstone School and transported his acolytes to the Windsor Park Nordic Centre. There he taught them how to ski. Over the years, the program evolved and expanded to include several city schools. Then, the Cross Country Ski Association of Manitoba came on board to develop a fundraiser known as "The Great Get Off Your Butt and Ski Corporate Relay".

CHRIS, AUGUST 13/09

> I had nice talks with Rilla, Mom and Win today. Jack Daniels called in the afternoon and we chatted for a while. It was raining lightly this morning so Sue and I just managed to sneak our walk in before the sun had broken completely through and warmed up too much. The rash on my face is much better and I will start reducing the use of the steroid cream. Little trials along the way.

I also spent some time answering e-mails today. We had a very nice walk and visit with Dianne and Karl tonight. We could not sit in the backyard as with no breeze, the mosquitoes were out. Tomorrow we will be at Cancer Care in the morning for blood tests. On Wednesday my blood values were holding more stable than for a while so maybe we will not need any blood products.

We are still adjusting to the new reality we are facing. I think we were both stronger today and beginning to work toward making the best of the upcoming days. One day at a time.

We look for the beauty in every day.

Kilcona Park

I'VE BEEN WALKING THE TRAILS HERE AT KILCONA PARK IN NORTH EAST Winnipeg. I wish I could say I was running them—in honour of Chris— but this isn't an easy course. I expected the trails to go around the hills but no, they wind over the top. It was an unrealistic expectation, knowing who designed the course. Yes, it was Chris McCubbins, and in his honour the site has been re-named The Chris McCubbins Cross Country Trails. Darren Klassen agreed on the level of difficulty.

It was interesting how Chris designed the course. It's very difficult. That's typical Chris. People are going to pay through running a difficult course. But, Chris never faltered. If there was a choice between an easy way and a hard one, Chris always took the hard way. If you are approaching a hill and there's a choice of going around or over, Chris always chose over.

The idea for a challenging cross country running trail—one that could be used in competitions—had been in the back of Chris' head for many years. Then he discovered Kilcona, a former dump site for the city of Winnipeg. The hills were just what he was looking for. When he appeared on the scene, seasonal city workers were cutting grass. Chris got to know these workers and shared his plan. Typical Chris, he had a plan. He mapped out the trail system and assisted the city staff in their work. He continued to groom the trails even after the grass cutters were laid off for the season. When the hired work crew returned in the spring, they were happy to know that they didn't have to start from scratch. They were also impressed with Chris' diligence and concern for the development of the park. As such, Chris managed the bureaucracy of city government by avoiding it. He knew that the city plan was to keep this as a park area and Chris developed a schematic plan of the trails for the walking, jogging and running community. Who could argue with that vision?

Later in the process, he would send out e-mail messages to the running community seeking their support and their strong backs. There was always weeding to be done or a monster pile of wood chips to be spread. It was physically demanding work—almost entirely manual labour.

Then trees and shrubs were planted—many with berries—food for the winged ones—plus maples that would provide colour in the fall and a shield for runners. Chris started many of the plants from cuttings and then filled in the gaps with excess stock donated by nurseries at the end of their selling year. Given that he was on good terms with the maintenance crew, he received their cooperation for grooming trails ensuring that the trees and shrubbery would be protected.

Chris said, "When I come here 20 years from now this is going to be quite a park."

CHRIS, AUGUST 14/09

As you can imagine it has been a very emotional day for us. We had a good cry this afternoon. We felt better afterward. Sue made an excellent dinner which I could eat. It helped that Dr Kumar had prescribed a mouth wash to deaden my tongue. The tongue continues to be a mystery. It has a sore that is so small no one can really see it, but I certainly feel it. This evening we had a beautiful walk around the neighbourhood and our spirits feel greatly buoyed. We have several things we need to do between now and whenever so that should help me to stay focused and find purpose.

We too often let wonderful relationships and time slip away.

CHRIS, AUGUST 15/09

Today has been a day at home. A mostly rainy day. The rain finally let up about 4:30 so we were able to go for an easy stroll. Sheldon and Karen were here at the time so we extended the visit by walking together. It is great to have so many wonderful people helping us during this time. It is a beautiful evening.

LIFE'S LITTLE ANNOYING INTERRUPTIONS DON'T STOP BECAUSE OF LIFE'S bigger crises. Inevitably, they keep happening. The following message from Chris is indicative of that reality.

CHRIS, AUGUST 16/09

The smoke detector for our Security System began to beep. Sue called and the lady tried to talk Sue through. The short form is that the batteries are special and of course in Winnipeg on a Sunday nothing is open until noon. They could not send out a tech for several days. The lady finally talked Sue through how to totally disconnect the system. The process was pretty hard on her. I went next door and our neighbour came over (he is pretty good with these things). He picked up some batteries after lunch and tried to get things restarted. After lunch Sue went to the Pan Am for a swim and I had a nap. Sue re-phoned the Security people because our system was still not working properly. They had her press the smoke alarm for almost a minute to restart things, which was pretty painful for Sue as sensitive as her hearing is. It did not work and they did not call back. Fortunately we went for a short walk with our neighbours and Bryan was able to figure what had been missed earlier. Not a very pleasant day for Sue.

I did talk with both my brothers and my sister. Mom was at Tip's but was resting when we talked. Sue is making dinner and we are both hoping for a relaxed evening.

CHRIS, AUGUST 17/09 MONDAY

We love all of you deeply and wish we had more time to reach out and give everyone a HUGE HUG. I know that because of the rapidity with which this disease has come back, I will not get to see many of you again. Please know that Sue and my love for you is as strong as if I could see you one last time.

Dreams

CHRIS LOVED TO DISAPPEAR IN THE WILDERNESS—AS FAR AWAY FROM civilization as possible—paddling, fishing, allowing nature to permeate his being. Stephen Riley remembered canoeing with Chris through the back woods, down long windy creeks and over blue lakes.

We camped on a small island across from an even smaller one— barely a rock outcrop with a few tall spruce on it. One of them was tall enough for an eagle's nest some 100 yards from our campsite— neighbours to the "baldies" and serenaded from time to time by the juveniles, screeching a chorus of "where's our food?" It was magical. At night, the loons would lullaby us into oblivion. In the day, we caught fish, ate shore lunches or plundered our packs for the best grub, scarfing trail mix as we paddled and portaged.

Chris was a fine canoeist, read the weather well, avoided un- necessary risks but was always up for a good challenge in the waves. He was steady, powerful, unruffled—totally laid back in the bush, but you knew you were with a guy who respected the perils of the forest—someone you could depend upon if the going got a bit dodgy or tough. He could read a compass like a wrist- watch. There were several occasions when he had to do just that. Out came the compass, then adjustments to our course and we were back on track—humping over rocks or struggling through sulphur-smelling swamps. And finally, pushing the boat out at our destination lake, that lopsided grin and chuckle: "Thought we wouldn't make it, huh?"

We'd take the portages slowly: stopping for blueberries, watch- ing whiskey jacks, enjoying the moment. Once, I was lying on my belly in a spruce glade, picking berries, plucking with both hands, munching, lost in the taste. I scraped ahead a foot or two and there, around a chunk of rock, I came eye to eye with a pink lady's slipper. I called Chris over with a stage whisper afraid to speak too loudly in fear that the blossom would wilt and die. He came over, knelt beside me and we both regarded that little orchid with awe. I can still remember his words "Isn't that the gift of our journey?

CHRIS, AUGUST 18/09 TUESDAY

We received many beautiful e-mails today. We would like to reply personally to each one but my energy is pretty low now and we had a very busy day. We had a wonderful walk this morning in the cool air after it stopped drizzling. In the late morning Sue had invited Phil and Donna, her pastor and his wife, over. We talked about many things and although at times very emotional we also found things to laugh about. At noon Brent Bottomley of the cross country ski association called to tell us they were renaming the Inner City Kids' Ski program and it's fundraiser in my honour. After finishing lunch and a nap, Jim Daly came by for a visit. While he was here Jim Lowe called from Vancouver. Just as Jim was leaving Karl and Dianne dropped off some food.

I had also talked with my brothers and mom in the morning. Tip and his wife Steffie will be arriving on Wednesday, Win will be arriving on Thursday provided he can get the flights arranged from London, Sue's dad and older brother, Ed, will be coming in on Friday, and my niece, KK, is expected Saturday. The next few days will be full of family so I will need to harbour my resources as much as possible. We are getting ready to go for our evening stroll to enjoy the fresh evening.

I feel blessed that I have been able to reconnect with many friends during this period. I only wish that I had made a greater effort earlier so we would have had more time. Reach out to someone you may have lost contact with. There is nothing more important than the relations you have and the love you can share.

CHRIS, AUGUST 19/09 WEDNESDAY 9:37 PM

We did I-Chat with Mom it was a lot of fun. It was such a new experience for her. Then began eating dinner. Tip and Steffie came over
while we were finishing dinner. They hooked up the I-Chat with
Mom. I was feeling pretty exhausted so I went up for another nap
while Tip, Steffie and Sue walked. We spent some time trying to
organize the eight drugs I am now on so I can keep it all straight.
I am hoping for a better sleep so I can enjoy Tip and Steffie more.

On August 20, Chris was admitted to Riverview Palliative Care ward.
He died at 1:00 pm on August 21, 2009.

Last Words

CHRIS DEVOTED A LARGE PART OF HIS LIFE TO RUNNING: POUNDING the pavements, hammering on tracks, gliding over grass, racing through forest trails, finding new paths in his journey—always pushing through the barrier of pain. As a result, his talents shone through. He was an All-American steeplechaser in College, Pan Am gold medalist, pentathlete, Olympic competitor and world class Masters Runner. But even after his days of competitive running were over, he continued to run, ski, lift weights, swim and bike. He had a life-long desire to be fit.

He also had a life-long passion for helping others—sharing his knowledge, helping kids to cope with life, instilling in them a sense of hope, sharing what he had with the less privileged and leaving a legacy of place—Kilcona Park for cross country runners and The Great Get Off Your Butt and Ski program for skiers.

The running and success of running gave him great highs not because he beat someone else but because he improved his own times. For his achievements, Chris was inducted into the Manitoba Sports Hall of Fame in 1999—one of his greatest treasures. In his memorabilia, there was the medal, tucked amongst the equally cherished cards from family, friends and fellow runners congratulating him on a life well run—recognizing such a key milestone of his athletic career.

He ran because he loved to run. In an interview with Chris Cariou of the *Winnipeg Free Press* in 1999, for the 20th Sports Hall of Fame Induction Ceremonies brochure, Chris summed up his philosophy.

It's been a wonderful rollercoaster ride. There have been frustrations where I sat and cried about what didn't happen, but it's the road to the gold. With the Pan Ams in Winnipeg, winning was great, but getting there was better.

During his battle with cancer there were times where optimism prevailed and down times when the bad news of his illness was overwhelming, but he endured these times just as he did in running.

When Chris entered the hospital for palliative care, there was no more need for planning—there was no hope for a cure—the race was over but, up to that point, he had fought the cancer with the same tenacity and the same strategy as he ran races. In running, he plotted his interval times; he kept track of the kinds and intensities of exercise; he researched best techniques; he stuck to a healthy diet regime; and he measured progress. When he entered the hospital, he organized a similar strategy. First he devoted a diary to the cause and titled the first page—"The New Adventure Begins." He drew rows and columns and plotted his counts for white blood cells, hemoglobin, platelets and oxygen and later on he recorded data on his vitals of temperature, blood pressure and pulse. He wrote details on how he felt, how he slept, who visited, what nurses were on call, how much exercising he did just like he did in the running diaries ("walked :35 around Churchill Drive" or "biked :42 around the neighbourhood")—the weather, the warm-up, the interval times and any aches and pains. Chris was plotting his progress to wellness and had full expectation that he was going to get better and better—just like his progress in running—improving steadily over time. He lived by the data. And, as he said, he was always able to "bounce back from past falls" but this one had proven more onerous.

Chris lived for every day. It didn't matter if he was out for a friendly run with his mates or competing against world-class runners. He enjoyed not only running but all the emotions attached to it. Chris wasn't living for next week or the week after that; he was living for the day. Near the end of his life, this philosophy of living became more apparent.

Communicating by e-mail, Chris kept his family and friends posted on his well-being. Ever the coach, there was a recurring theme. People are important. Take the time to reconnect. Don't lose track of your friends. In his words,

> I feel blessed that I have been able to reconnect with many friends during this period. I only wish that I had made a greater effort earlier so we would have had more time. Reach out to someone you may have lost contact with. There is nothing more important than the relations you have and the love you can share.

Appendix I

CHRIS McCUBBINS: A SAMPLE OF RACES

DATE	LOCATION	MEET	RACE	TIME	PLACE	WINNING TIME
October 3, 1964	OSU Hillcrest, Stillwater, Oklahoma	X-C	X-C 3-mile	14:59	5/49	John Camien Emporia State 14:45.3
November 7, 1964	Manhattan, Kansas	Big Eight Conference X-C Meet	X-C 3-mile	14:43	7/54	Dave Wighton Colorado Univ. 14:12
February 24, 1965	Kansas City	Big Eight 37th annual	2-mile		3rd	
May 1, 1965	OSU Hillcrest	OSU-OU Dual Track Meet	1-mile		2nd	Tom Von Ruden 4:15.4
			3-mile	14:56.2	3-way tie for First place	14:56.2
May 16, 1965	Manhattan, Kansas	Big Eight All Sports	3-mile	14:14.2	2nd	John Lawson, KU 14:09.6 (new record)
October 9, 1965	OSU Hillcrest	OSU Jamboree	4-mile	20:31	8/49	George Scott New Mexico 19:33.3
October 23, 1965	OSU Hillcrest	Arkansas at Stillwater	3-mile	14:54	1st	
November 6, 1965	OSU Hillcrest	Big Eight Conference X-C Meet	3-mile	14:58.0	14/53	John Lawson Kansas Univ. 14:04.3

DATE	LOCATION	MEET	RACE	TIME	PLACE	WINNING TIME
November 22, 1965	University of Kansas, Lawrence, Kansas	27th National Collegiate X-C Championships	6-mile	30:07	5/152	John Lawson Kansas U 29:24

DATE	LOCATION	MEET	RACE	TIME	PLACE	WINNING TIME
February 20, 1966	Lawrence, Kansas, Allen Field House	Triangular Meet	2-mile		2nd	John Lawson, KU 8:59.8, a new meet Record. Old meet record, 9:13. Old field house record, 9:05.

DATE	LOCATION	MEET	RACE	TIME	PLACE	WINNING TIME
February 26, 1966	Kansas City, Missouri	Big Eight Indoor Championships	2-mile	9:12.9	2nd	John Lawson KU 9:08.5

DATE	LOCATION	MEET	RACE	TIME	PLACE	WINNING TIME
March 19, 1966	Manhattan, Kansas	Big Eight	2-mile		2nd	Nelson St. Cloud 8:59.2

DATE	LOCATION	MEET	RACE	TIME	PLACE	WINNING TEAM
March 26, 1966	Fayetteville, Arkansas	Arkansas Relays	2-mile Relay	7:38.6	1st	Arnold Droke Chris McCubbins Jim Metcalf Tom Von Ruden
			4-mile Relay	17:29.8	1st	Glenn Blakley Ray Smith Chris McCubbins Tom Von Ruden

DATE	LOCATION	MEET	RACE	TIME	PLACE	WINNING TIME
April 1, 1966	Austin, Texas	39th Annual Texas Relays	Distance Medley	9:48.2	5th	Abilene at 9:36.5 just 1.5 Seconds above the world record for this race.

DATE	LOCATION	MEET	RACE	TIME	PLACE	OTHER TIMES / WINNING TIME
April 9, 1966	OSU Hillcrest	Arkansas Dual	3000-metre Steeplechase	9:00.2	1st	OTHER TIMES: Von Ruden came in 2nd and Tip McCubbins was 3rd
April 16, 1966	Columbia, Mo Memorial Stadium	Missouri Dual At Columbia	3-mile	14:15.8	1st	WINNING TIME
April 22, 1966	Lawrence, Kansas	Kansas Relays	Open 3000-metre Steeplechase	9:23.4	3rd	WINNING TIME: Hylke Van ber Wal, a runner from Manitoba was first at 9:09.5
April 29, 1966	Des Moines, Iowa	57th Annual Drake Relays	2-mile	9:02.4	3rd	WINNING TIME: 8:46 Oscar Moore, Southern Illinois, a record. The old record 8:51.3
May 5, 1966	Stillwater Lewis Stadium Oval, OSU	52nd Annual OSU – OU Dual Meet	3-mile	14:30.8	1st	WINNING TIME: Track record. Old record by Glenn Blakley, 1964 @ 14:31 Meet record. The old Meet record of 14:56.2 by Chris McCubbins, Glenn Blakley and Ray Smith from 1965.
			1-mile	4:20.3	1st	
May 13, 1966	Columbia, Mo Memorial Stadium	Big Eight Track Championship	3-mile	14:03.9	1st	WINNING TIME: New record. Old: John Lawson Kansas 1965

DATE	LOCATION	MEET	RACE	TIME	PLACE	WINNING TIME
June 16, 1966	Bloomington, Indiana	45th annual NCAA Track Championships	3000-metre Steeplechase		4th	
October 1, 1966	OSU Hillcrest	OSU X-C Jamboree	4-mile X-C	19:34	2/36	19:18.3 George Scott New Mexico
November 5, 1966	Iowa State Golf course Ames, Iowa	Big Eight Conference X-C Meet	3-mile	14:16.9	1/52	
March 4, 1967	Kansas Municipal Auditorium	Big Eight Indoor Track Meet	2-mile	9:02.2	1st	Meet record previously 9:03.1 set by Miles Eiserman, OSU 1959
March 10, 1967		NCAA Indoors	2-mile	8:52.4	5th	Gerry Lindgren Washington State U 8:31.6
March 29, 1967	Houston, Texas	Triangular Meet Rice/OSU/Lamar Tech	1-mile	4:07.8	1st	
April 1, 1967	Austin, Texas	Big Eight Texas Relays	3-mile	13:38.7	1st	

DATE	LOCATION	MEET	RACE	TIME	PLACE	WINNING TIME
April 8, 1967	Lawrence, Kansas	43nd Annual Kansas Relays	3000-metre Steeplechase	8:46.6	1st	New Kansas Relays record Old record: 8:56.3 by HylkeVan Der Wal, 1964
April 29, 1967	Des Moines, Iowa	Drake Relays	2-mile	8:53.4	2nd	8:51.1 George Scott New Mexico
May, 1967	Oklahoma	5th Annual Oklahoma Christian College Relays	2-mile	9:11.2	1st	Beats the Meet record by 21.2 seconds.
May 4, 1967	OSU Hillcrest	OU-OSU Meet	1-mile	4:14.2	1st Tie	Tie with teammate Tom Laubert
			3-mile	14:09.3	1st	Beating Chris' old meet record of 14:30.8 of 1966.
May 20, 1967	OSU Hillcrest	Big Eight Conference T & F Meet	3-mile	13:51.9	1st	Knocked 12 seconds off his last year's time
June 15-17, 1967	Provo, Utah Brigham Young University Stadium	46th Annual NCAA Track & Field Championships (National College Athletics Association)	3000-metre Steeplechase	8:51.4	1st	OTHER TIMES New national record. Old, 9:27.4 and a Stadium record.

DATE	LOCATION	MEET	RACE	TIME	PLACE	WINNING TIME / OTHER TIMES
June 23, 1967	Bakersfield, CA	AAU track & Field Championships	3000-metre Steeplechase	9:02.0	6th	Pat Traynor, US Air Force 8:42.0
July 23, 1967	Minneapolis, Minnesota	Pan-Am Games Trials	3000-metre Steeplechase	8:39.6	1st	National Collegiate Record
July 15-16, 1967	Winnipeg, University of Manitoba Stadium	5th Pan-American Games	3000-metre Steeplechase	8:38.2	1st	Pan-Am record Canadian record
August 10, 1967	Montreal Autostade	America vs. Europe Track & Field Meet	3000-metre Steeplechase	8:44.1	1st	
January 1, 1968	Saskatoon, SK	Saskatchewan Centennial Indoor Games	2-mile	9:06.2	2nd	George Scott Australia 9:02.4
April 13, 1968	Norman, Oklahoma	John Jacobs Invitational	3000-metre Steeplechase	9:12.3	2nd	Conrad Nightingale 9:07.1
April 18-20, 1968	Lawrence, Kansas	43nd Kansas Relays	10,000-metre	31:36.8	5th	Jim Murphy 29:51.6
			3000-metre Steeplechase	8:59.8	2nd	Conrad Nightingale 8:52.8
Spring 1968	Monroe LA Civic Arena	Inaugural North-east Boosters Club Indoor Meet	2-mile	8:52.8	1st	

DATE	LOCATION	MEET	RACE	TIME	PLACE	WINNING TIME
June 29, 1968	South Lake Tahoe Coliseum	United States Olympic track & field trials	3000-metre Steeplechase	9:37.4	8th	8:57.9 George Young Casa Grande
July 19, 1969	Wichita Falls, Texas	Sheppard Inter Service track & field Championships	3000-metre Steeplechase	8:59.1	1st	A new Sheppard Record but 2 seconds short of AAU Qualifying time.
Tuesday, July 8, 1969	Cork, Ireland 'Mardyke'	Cork City Sports Meet	5000-metre	13:55.4	1st	This was a personal best for Chris in this race.

April 17-18, 1970 — Fox-catcher Farms Media, Penn. — 4th Triathlon Invitational & National Championships

EVENT	TIME	POINTS	PLACE	OVERALL
Swim	2:46	872	27/51	1st with 3293 points
Shoot		180/800	12/51	
Run	10:48	1621	1/51	

July 13, 1970 — Fort Sam Houston, Texas — Modern Pentathlon National Championships

EVENT	TIME	POINTS	PLACE	OVERALL
Ride		1000	5/23	2743 points
Fence		875		
Shoot		868		

May 3, 1970 — Fort Sam Houston, Texas

EVENT	TIME	POINTS	PLACE	OVERALL
Swim	2:42	904	11/36	2nd with 3148 points
Shoot	13:02	980	3/35	
Run		1264	1/35	

DATE	LOCATION	MEET	RACE	TIME	PLACE	WINNING TIME
August 21-22, 1970	University of Manitoba Stadium	Canadian Senior & Junior Track & Field Championships	3000-metre Steeplechase	8:49.0	1st	

DATE	LOCATION	MEET	RACE	TIME	PLACE	WINNING TIME
First weekend of August 1970	Winnipeg Beach To Gimli	Icelandic Festival Run	10-mile	52.7.1	1st	
1971				52.31.8	1st	
1972				54.44.0	1st	
1975				48:24	1st	
1979				55:56	1st	
1981				48:55	1st	
1989				53:14	1st	
DATE	LOCATION	MEET	RACE	TIME	PLACE	WINNING TIME
July 6, 1974	Griffiths Stadium, Saskatoon		5000-metre	14:12.4	1st	Outdoor native senior record
DATE	LOCATION	MEET	RACE	TIME	PLACE	WINNING TIME
October 27, 1973	Regina, SK	Prairie Regional X-C Meet		46:08	1st	
DATE	LOCATION	MEET	RACE	TIME	PLACE	WINNING TIME
November 16, 1974	Brock University St. Catharines, ON	Canadian X-C Championships	Open Men 12,000-metre	34:17	4th	Neil Cusak, Ireland, 33:23.2
DATE	LOCATION	MEET	RACE	TIME	PLACE	WINNING TIME
November 30, 1974	Belmont, CA	National AAU X-C	10,000-metre	31:05.9	18/270	John Ngeno (WSU) 29:58.8
DATE	LOCATION	MEET	RACE	TIME	PLACE	WINNING TIME
May 27, 1975	Winnipeg Pan-Am Stadium	MTFA Twilight	10,000-metre	29:24.6	1st	
June 24, 1975			10,000-metre	30:10.4	1st	
June 25, 1975			5000-metre	14:24.2	1st	
July 29, 1975			1500-metre	3:50.0	1st	

DATE	LOCATION	MEET	RACE	TIME	PLACE	WINNING TIME
July 19, 1975	Pan-Am Stadium	Manitoba Track & Field Championships	5,000-metre	14:36.6	1st	
July 18, 1975			3000-metre Steeplechase	8:51.8	1st	
July 25, 1975	Kent Park Montreal	Canadian Open	10,000-metre	28:16.51	6th	Miruts Yifter (Ethiopia) 28:09.14 The next 4 runners were from Mexico, Rome & Belgium.
July 29, 1975	Pan-Am Stadium Winnipeg	Local	1500-metre	3:50.0	1st	Outdoor native senior record for Manitoba
August 12, 1975	Regina	Western Canada Summer Games	3000-metre Steeplechase	8:59.0	1st	
August 13			5000-metre	14:12.2	1st	
August 22-24, 1975	Sudbury, ON	National T & F Championships	10,000-metre	29:25.2	3rd	
August 24			5000-metre	14:15.0	5th	
August 26, 1975	Laurentian University Sudbury, ON	Men's Invitational T & F Competition	3000-metre	8:09.2	1st	Manitoba outdoor open & Native record.
August 29, 1975	Laurentian University Sudbury, ON	Men's Invitational T & F Competition	5000-metre	14:08.8	5th	Jerome Drayton 13:40.6

DATE	LOCATION	MEET	RACE	TIME	PLACE	WINNING TIME / WINNING RUNNER
September 14, 1975	University of Manitoba Stadium (440 yard Tartan Track)	Manitoba Track & Field	Invitational 20-km Track Race	1:02:25.	1st	Manitoba Open & Native Record American Open & Native Record Canadian Open Record
November 15, 1975	Vancouver, BC Stanley Park	Canadian X-C Championships	Open Men 12,000-metre	37:28.4	1/74	
December 30, 1975	Saskatoon		2-mile	8:46.1	2nd	Paul Cummings
February 14, 1976	Winnipeg Arena	Knights of Columbus Indoor Games	3000-metre	8:17.0	3rd	Ron Martin, Gr. Br. 8:02.0
March 19, 1976	Marian College, California		3-mile	13:44.6	1st	
April 1, 1976	Austin, Texas		10,000-metre	29:01.2	3rd	
April 2, 1976			5000-metre	13:55.64	2nd	
April 24, 1976	Des Moines, Iowa	Drake Relays	10,000-metre	28:28.63	4th	Ed Mendoza 28:23.15
April 23, 1976			5000-metre	13:51.8	2nd	

DATE	LOCATION	MEET	RACE	TIME	PLACE	WINNING TIME
May 8, 1976	Knoxville, Tennessee	Tom Black Classic	5000-metre	13:44.8	2nd	Mike Keogh (NYAC) 13:39.1. Beats the old track record of 13:46.1. Chris in 2nd place also beats the record.
May 29, 1976	Laval, Quebec	Olympic Trials	10,000-metre	29:29.0	1st	
May 30, 1976			5000-metre	14:27	3rd	
July 23, 1976	Montreal	Olympic Games	10,000-metre Heat	33:22.35	12th	
December 30, 1976	Saskatoon Arena		3000-metre	8:10.0	1st	Manitoba indoor native Senior men record
October 23, 1977	Saskatoon	Prairie 12,000-metre X-C Championships	X-C	38:51	1st	
November 12, 1977	Hull, Quebec	Canadian Cross Country Championships	X-C	38:27.08	1/118	
October 22, 1978	Regina Top Hill Golf Course	1978 Prairie X-C Championships	Open 12,000-metre	36.45	2nd	1st Peter Butler Alberta 36.38.3

DATE	LOCATION	MEET	RACE	TIME	PLACE	WINNING TIME
November 4, 1978	High Park, Toronto University of Toronto	CIAU X-C Championships	10,000-metre	32:48	3rd	Paul Williams U of T 31:10
November 18, 1978	Stanley Park Vancouver, B.C.	Canadian X-C Championships	12,000-metre	37:26	10/108	Peter Butler 36:35.8
May 25, 1980	Winnipeg (outdoors)	Winnipeg Tribune 'Run for Fun'	10,000-metre	30:06	1st	
May 24, 1981	Winnipeg Outdoors	Athletes Wear 'Run for Fun'	10,000-metre Road Race	29:46	1st	
May 16, 1982				29:38	1st	
May, 1986				30:39	1st	
June 4, 1989				31:02	1st	
August 30, 1981	Birds Hill Park, Manitoba	Labatt's 20-K	20,000-metre	62:42	3rd	1st Jerry Kooymans, Toronto 61:52
May 1, 1982	Fargo, North Dakota	Pepsi Challenge	10,000-metre	30:03	1st	
March 27, 1983	St. Vital Park, Winnipeg	Puma 5-K	5000-metre	15:02	1st	
April 10, 1983	Kildonan Park, Winnipeg	Puma 10-K	10,000-metre	30:06	1st	
April 24, 1983	Assiniboine Park, Winnipeg	Puma 15-K	15,000-metre	45:43	1st	
April 30, 1989	Assiniboine Park, Winnipeg	Puma 15-K	15,000-metre	49:36	3rd	

DATE	LOCATION	MEET	RACE	TIME	PLACE	WINNING TIME
February 4, 1984	Beacon Hill Park, Victoria, B.C.	Canadian X-C Championships	7.5-mile	37:04.5	5th	1st Paul McCoy 36:17.2 (Newfoundland)
February 1984	Saanichton, British Columbia	Nike-Molson Vancouver Island Series	8000-metre	24:07.2	3rd Open Category 1st in Pre-Masters	1st Brian Rhodes 23:43.2
May 31, 1984	Spokane, Washington	Bloomsday Run 12-K	12,000-metre	36:59	1st 35-39 Age Category	19th overall
June 10, 1984	St. Gabriel-de-Brandon, Quebec	Maski-Courons 20-K	20,000-metre	1:04.28.2	4th	1st Dave Edge 1:03.16.0
February 1986	Winnipeg	Boeing Indoor Track Classic	3000-metre	8:24	1st	
August 26, 1986	Manitoba	Birds Hill 20-K	20,000-metre	63:02	2nd Open 1st 40-44 Class	1st Open Bob Cook 62:56

MASTERS RUNS

DATE	LOCATION	MEET	RACE	TIME	PLACE	WINNING TIME
June 29, 1986	Portland, Oregon	Cascade Run-Off	15-K	46:06.75	1st in Masters	
August 9, 1986	New Jersey	Asbury Park 10-K	10-K	30:49	1st in Masters	
June 30, 1987	Portland, Oregon	Cascade Run-Off	15-K	45:34.84	1st in Masters	New North American Record
July 12, 1987		Western Canada Game Trials	10-K	30:34.0	2nd	1st in Masters Rob guy 30:08.2
August 8, 1987	New Jersey	Asbury Park 10-K	10-K	30:57	1st in Masters	
August 16, 1987	Cape Cod	Falmouth Road Race		34:34	1st in Masters	
January 10, 1988	Winnipeg		Indoor 5-K	14:40.1	1st in Men 40-44	A new Canadian Masters Athletic Association Record for the Men 40-44 category.
June 18, 1989	Portland, Oregon	Cascade Run-Off	15-K	46:43.90	3rd in Masters	1st Masters Wilson Waigwa 46:08.34 (Kenya)
August 27, 1989	Manitoba	Birds Hill 20 K	20-K	1:05.44	1st	

DATE	LOCATION	MEET	RACE	TIME	PLACE	WINNING TIME
October 7, 1989	Maple Grove Park, Manitoba	Manitoba Senior X-Country Championships	10-K	32:03	1st	
1991	Grand Beach, Manitoba	Grand Prix Sun Run	10-K	33:17	2nd (1st in 45-49 Class)	Open 1st Chris Glowak 32:58
July 24, 1991	Selkirk, Manitoba	Catfish Classic	5-K	15:50	3rd Open 1st in over (45-49)	Darcy Ready, Open 1st 15:40
September 8, 1991	Winnipeg	Run for Chiropractic	10-K	32:18	5th Open 1st in over 40	Chris Weber 31:09

Appendix 2

RECORDS

APRIL 30, 1979, MANITOBA TRACK & FIELD ASSOCIATION, OUTDOOR RECORDS

Here are the records held by Chris McCubbins as of April 30, 1979. The 10,000 metre record of 28:16 is still in place as of June 2013.

EVENT	CATEGORY	RECORD TIME	DATE SET	PLACE	OTHER
1500-metre	Native Record	3:50.0	July 29, 1975	Winnipeg	Tom Von Ruden sets the Open record at 3:43.3, USA, August 2, 1967

EVENT	CATEGORY	RECORD TIME	DATE SET	PLACE	OTHER
3000-metre	Native & Open Record	8:09.2	August 26, 1975	Sudbury	

EVENT	CATEGORY	RECORD TIME	DATE SET	PLACE	OTHER
5000-metre	Native & Open Record	13:44.8	May 8, 1976	Knoxville, Tenn.	

EVENT	CATEGORY	RECORD TIME	DATE SET	PLACE	OTHER
10,000-metre	Native & Open Record	28:16.6	July 25, 1975	Montreal	

EVENT	CATEGORY	RECORD TIME	DATE SET	PLACE	OTHER
3000-metre Steeplechase	Open Record	8:38.2	July 30, 1967	Winnipeg	
	Native Record	8:40.8	June 17, 1972	Seattle	

Sources of Information

ARTICLES

"Pop Fare for a Popular Fair," by John Underwood, *Sports Illustrated*, August 21, 1967.

"Chris McCubbins (1945–2009): Role Model," by Dean Tweed, *Canadian Runner*, December 22, 2009.

BOOKS

"Daniels' Running Formula," by Dr. Jack Daniels, *Human Kinetics*, Champaign, IL, 1998.

Outliers: The Story of Success by Malcolm Gladwell, Little, Brown and Company, New York 2008.

BROCHURES AND NEWSLETTERS

Canadian Track & Field Olympic Trials '72, July 22-23, 1972

Cascade Run-Off, Portland,Oregon, June 28, 1987

Cascade Run-Off, Portland, Oregon, June 18, 1989

Commencement Ceremonies, Oklahoma State University, May 26, 1968

15th Annual Falmouth Road Race, August 16, 1987

Drake Relays, 67th Annual, Track & Field Results, April 24, 1976

Higgins of OSU, Oklahoma State, tribute to Coach Higgins, 1967

Manitoba Sports Hall of Fame, 20th Annual Induction Ceremonies, November 13, 1999, Winnipeg, Manitoba

Manitoba Track & Field Association Outdoor Records, April 30, 1979

46th NCAA Track & Field Championships, June 15-16-17, BYU Stadium, Provo, Utah

Official Programs, Islendingadagurinn, Gimli Manitoba, 1970–1991

Official Program, 5th Pan-American Games, Aug. 1967 Pan Am
    Games, Winnipeg Canada
OSU *Daily O'Collegian*, January 13, 1967
OSU *Daily O'Collegian*, February 23, 1967
United States Modern Pentathlon Team, Information, Fort Sam
    Houston, Texas

CERTIFICATES
All-American College Track and Field Team, June 18, 1966
All-American College Track and Field Team, June 17, 1967
Birth, Chris McCubbins
Certificate of Award, V Pan-American Games, first place, 3000-metre
    steeplechase, August 7, 1967
Honorable Discharge, from the Armed forces of the United States of
    America, December 1974
Province of Manitoba, National Honours award, 1974

DIARIES
Sue Jacobsen, Travel to South East Asia and South Pacific, October
    1/1990 to July 31, 1991
Sue Jacobsen, February 2, 2008 - August 17, 2009
Chris McCubbins, Running Diaries 1972 – 1986
Chris McCubbins, The New Adventure Begins, February 17, 2009,
    Chris' daily progress report of treatment, observations and med-
    ical records

E-MAIL CORRESPONDENCE
Rilla Chaney
Charlie Christmas
Jack Daniels
Dick Fosbury
Rosemary Krushel
Phil McCubbins
Tip McCubbins
Jim Metcalf

Sheldon Reynolds
Mavis Riley
Stephen Riley
Ray Smith
Grant Towns

FAMILY HISTORY AND PERSONAL STORIES
Ancestors of Raymond Christopher McCubbins, a family tree printout
I Remember Chris the Educator, Grace Parson
McCubbin Line of Descent, unknown origin
Memories of our Friend and Mentor, Chris by Kim & Randy Longmuir
Oral History of the McCubbins/Snider Families, by Juanita Snider
 McCubbins, transcribed by Julia Ross
Recollections of Canoeing with Chris, April 23, 2012, Stephen Riley
Thinking of Chris, Carole & Joe Mackintosh
Untitled by Iris Muirhead
Untitled by Susan Jacobsen

INTERVIEWS BY THE AUTHOR
Jim Daly, May 10, 2011
Greg Gemmell, May 24, 2011
Marie Mackintosh, July 8, 2012
Sue Jacobsen, May 31, 2010, June 1, 2010, September 14, 2010
Darren Klassen, June 17, 2012
Rilla Chaney, September 17, 2012
Sheldon Reynolds, July 6, 2010, November 9, 2010, July 4, 2012
Dianne Sproll, May 31, 2011
Karl Sproll, May 31, 2011
Bruce Soulsby, June 16, 2011
Grant Towns, June 9, 2011

LETTERS TO CHRIS
Amateur Athletic Union of the United States, Selection to the inter-
 national track & field team, July 28, 1967
Ivan Biblow, Letter of Recommendation, April 21, 1983

John Buchanan, Letter of Recommendation, April 7, 1983
Court of Canadian Citizenship, January 27, 1976
Jack Daniels, October 28, 1966, Effects of altitude on runners
Laurent Desjardins, Minister of Health and Social Development,
     Province of Manitoba, Congratulatory letter, July 16, 1978
Charles A Galford, Congratulatory letter, July 30, 1987
Peter Gzowski, Remembering the radio chat, November 25, 1999.
Ralph Higgins, OSU coach, January 16, 1978
Robert B. Kamm, President OSU, congratulations, November 8, 1966
Letter of thanks from the parent of a student, June 30, 1987
Chris McCubbins, letter to family on the back of an army photo,
     December 1968
US Army, Relieved from Active Duty Notice, September 2, 1970

NEWSPAPER CLIPPINGS (IN ORDER OF APPEARANCE IN THE TEXT)
Enid Daily Eagle, November 23, 1965
Ibid, February 6, 1966
Topeka Capital Journal, February 27, 1966
Daily Oklahoman, March 1966
Ibid, April 2, 1966
Enid Morning News, April 27, 1967
Oklahoman Journal, May 5, 1967
Deseret News, June 17, 1967
Enid Morning News, August 27, 1967
Winnipeg Free Press, January 1, 1968
The Sunday Oklahoman, April 13, 1968
Kansas City Times, April 19, 1968
Enid Morning News, March 8, 1970
Enid Daily Eagle, April 21, 1970
Winnipeg Free Press, August 14, 1975
Regina Leader Post, August 14, 1975
Winnipeg Free Press, February 12, 1976
Enid News Eagle, March 1976
Winnipeg Free Press, October 10, 1978
Winnipeg Tribune, May 28, 1980

Winnipeg Free Press, November 1985
Asbury Park Press, August 10, 1986
Cape Cod Times, August 17, 1987
Winnipeg Free Press, June 5, 1989

TAPED INTERVIEWS
Peter Gzowski, CBC Morningside, radio broadcast week of July 26, 1976
Juanita McCubbins, fall 2010, interviewed by Sue Jacobsen

TELEPHONE CONVERSATIONS
Rilla Chaney, April 26, 2012; June 20, 2012, July 12, 2012
Marie Mackintosh, May 3, 2012
Rosemary Krushel, June 5, 2012, June 17, 2012
Iris Muirhead, May 13, 2012
Tom Von Ruden, December 5, 2011

OTHER
"Chisholm Trail," from the digital library Encyclopedia of Oklahoma History and Culture
"Chisholm Trail," from online, Texas State Historical Association
CN Telegram, August 9, 1967
Jack Daniels, Thirsty Thursday Video, Season 7, Episode 5, "Jack's Biggest Accomplishment."
E-mail messages, Chris McCubbins 2009
History of the Modern Pentathlon, Oxford University, Modern Pentathlon Association
Manitoba Track & Field Association Report, April 30, 1979
Manitoba Swimming Championships Results, January 1982 p. 69
"Results & Analysis of High Altitude Training," Jack Daniels 1968
Teacher Performance Reviews, John A Buchanan, 1976, 1977
Teacher Evaluation Report, J. Hamm, April 13, 1978
US Army Identification Card

Acknowledgements

MY THANKS TO THE MANY PEOPLE WHO PROVIDED INFORMATION AND anecdotes—often filling in the gaps on the time-line and always enriching the story. Particular thanks to Sue Jacobsen, Rilla Chaney, Sheldon Reynolds and my sister Marie—all sources of information and most often inspiration that allowed me to finish the task.

I enjoyed corresponding with the OSU team, people who ran with Chris in his college days. Ray Smith provided details on races and lots of photographs. He also put me in touch with others—colleagues of Chris on the running adventure.

I was in Australia during the editing stages and thank Ray and Ted Stuckey for their hospitality and especially for the use of Ted's office and computer. Good on ya!

As usual, my family were invaluable in their support and assistance: for Carole for her encouragement, collabration and diligence in reading drafts, for my brother Ord for his fond recollections of Chris, and for Karen and Josh, Heather and Anthony, and John and Erin for their presence and for their support in the process.

Index

Abilene rail yards, 17
Adelaide, Australia, 122
Alamosa, Colorado, 41–43, *ill*, 125–126
All-American College Track and Field
  Team, 28, 45
All American Cross Country Team, 21, 22
Amateur Athletic Union, 45, 66
American Athletic Association, 70
American Athletic Union, 47, 52
Ames, Iowa, 26–27
Arkansas Dual, 28
Asbury Park, 114, 115–116
Assiniboine Park, 47, 82, 102, 106, 117
Athletes Wear races, 103, 113, 116, 117
Austin, Texas, 23, 39, 85–86
Australia, 122
Autostade (Montreal), 47

Badgley, Wayne, 25
Bakersfield, California, 45
Bali, Indonesia, 121
Bangkok, Thailand, 121
Beacon Hill Park (Victoria), 106
Belilgne, Atlaw, 116
Bell, Wade, 42, 45
Belmont, California, 70
Besson, Allan, 75, 112
Biblow, Ivan, 105
Big Eight Conference, 20, 22, 25, 26,
  27–28, 39, *ill*
Billings, Oklahoma, 31
Birds Hill Park, 97, 104
Birds Hill race, 117
Bisons (University of Manitoba), 97

Blakley, Glenn, *ill*
Bloomington, Indiana, 28
Bloomsday Run, 107
Boeing Indoor Track Classic, 112
Booth, Michael, *ill*
Boston, Massachusetts, 51–52
Boston, Ralph, 45, 52
Bottomley, Brent, 137
boxing, grandfather and, 30
Brandon, Manitoba, 96
Brigham Young University Stadium, 43,
  44–45, *ill*
Bright, Jerry, 48
Brock University, 70
Buchanan, John A., 71, 73, 105–106
Bunch, Wayne, 85

Cable, Richard, 19
Canadian Broadcasting Corporation
  (CBC), 91–93
Canadian Cross Country
  Championships, 70, 78, 96, 106
Canadian Cross Country team, in
  Scotland, 96
Canadian National Track and Field
  Championships, 76–77
Canadian Olympic Trials, 87
Canadian Open Olympic Trials, 66, 74
Canadian Senior & Junior Track &
  Field Championships, 66
CANSI (Canadian Association of
  Nordic Ski Instructors), 16
Cape Cod, Massachusetts, 116
Cardinal Swim Club, 102

Cariou, Chris, 139
Carlos, John, 45
Casa Grande, 100
Cascade Run-Off, 113–115, 117
Chaney, Anne (niece), *ill*
Chaney, Marvin (brother-in-law), 69, 81, *ill*
Chaney, Nathania (niece), *ill*
Chaney, Rilla M. (née McCubbins) (sister), 18, 25, 32–33, *ill*, 58, 85, *ill*, 121, 123–124; and CM's illness, 69, 80, 81, 107, 128, 132
Charleswood In Motion, 103
Chicago, Illinois, 29
China, 121
Chisholm Trail, 17
Christmas, Charlie, 23, 24
church, parents' involvement with, 32
Churchill Drive, 119
Clemmons, Mary Frances (great-great-grandmother), 29
Columbia, Missouri, 25
Columbus, Missouri, 38
Cork City Sports Meet, 60
Council of International Military Sports (CISM), 58, 62
Cowboys (OSU team, a.k.a. Pokes), 20, 23, 24
Creston, British Columbia, 121
Cross Country Jamboree, 20
Cross Country Ski Association of Manitoba, 132
Cub Scouts, 32, *ill*
Cusak, Neil, 70

Daily O'Collegian, 27, 38
Daily Oklahoman, 23–24
Daly, Jim, 64–65, 69, 137
Daniels, Jack: on runner's success, 28; fitness testing, 41–42, 125–126; and high-altitude training, 43, 84–85; and modern pentathlon, 57, 63; influence of, 65, 84–85, 118; on CM's sportsmanship in Montreal, 91; and timing of CM's running career, 129

David Livingstone School, Winnipeg, 123–124, 132
Denman, Lillie May (great-grandmother) *See* McCubbins, Lillie May
Des Moines, Iowa, 86–87
Drake Relays, 40, 84, 86
drugs in sport, 115, 129
Du Pont, John, 62
Dusseldorf, Germany, 48

Edge, David, 104, 107
Eiserman, Miles, 39
Eisler, Dale, 76
Ellis, Iris, 34
Emerson, Manitoba, 63
Enid Daily Eagle, 21–22
Enid High School, 18–19, 20, 21, 22, 38, *ill*
Enid Morning News, 22
Enid News Eagle, 85
Enid, Oklahoma: in CM's early years, 17–19, 20, 21–22, 32, 49, *ill*, 111; in CM's adulthood, 54–55, 69, 80, 85, *ill*
Europe vs. Americas Track and Field Meet, 47
European Games, 48
Ewoma (Registered Clinical Assistant), 130
Expo 67, 47–48

Falmouth Road Race, 116
Farah, Mohamed, 99
Farmer, Larry, *ill*
Fayetteville, Arkansas, 23
Feathers, Jim, *ill*
Flagstaff, Arizona, 84
Fleming, Mike, 26
Ford, Phil, 40
Fort Polk, Louisiana, 56, 58, *ill*
Fort Sam Houston, Texas, 58, 61, 62, 63
Fosbury, Dick, 43
Fosbury flop, 43–44
Foxcatcher Farms, 61–62
Frank Kennedy Centre, 65
French, Ken, 75

Fresno, California, 23
Frodo (dog), 66–68, 97, *ill*
Fulton, Vic, 17–18

Galford, Charles A. "Chuck", 115
Gates, Bill, as example, 128–129
GD6 (adult oncology/bone marrow
    transplant ward), 16, 82, 130
Gemmell, Greg, 14–15, 102, 103, 107,
    ill, 116, 117
Gili Air, Indonesia, 121
Gimli, Manitoba, 14–15, 68, 103, 116
Gladwell, Malcolm, 128
Grand Forks, North Dakota, 54
The Great Get Off Your Butt and Ski
    Program, *ill*, 130, 132, 139
Great Land Run, 29–30
Greenwood Place, 99, 101, 102
Greer, Doug, *ill*
Gritty Grotto, 65
Gzowski, Peter, 91–92

Halifax, Nova Scotia, 96
Hamm, J., 97
Health Sciences Centre, Winnipeg, 16,
    82
Heinonen, Tom, 42
Higgins, Ralph, 19–20, 22, 23, 64–65,
    ill; on CM as greatest two-miler, 22,
    27; steeplechase practice and, 28
high jump, 43–44
Hillcrest cross country course, 20, 26, *ill*
Hong Kong, 121
Houston, Texas, 39
Howard, Tom, 75–76
Hull, Quebec, 96
Hurd, Mike, 113, 114, 116

Inaugural North-East Boosters Club, 52
Indonesia, 121
Islendingadagurinn (Icelandic Race),
    116, 117

Jacobsen, Ed (brother-in-law), 137
Jacobsen, Jim (brother-in-law), 100, 121

Jacobsen, Sue (second wife): first years
    with CM, 100–107; as physiother-
    apist, 100, 101, 129; moves to Victoria
    and back, 105, 107; runs competitive-
    ly, 113, 116, 117; investigates person-
    ality type, 110; at home with CM,
    ill; keeps garden, 119; travels around
    Pacific Rim with CM, 121–122; learns
    CM's diagnosis, 15–16; visits Enid,
    80, *ill*; bakes and cooks, 108, 134,
    135; deals with smoke alarm, 135;
    explores spirituality, 127–128, 137;
    practises Touch of Healing, 127; plays
    crib with Tip, 108; walks, 107, 132,
    135, 138; marriage to CM, 69, 81; at
    tree planting, *ill*
Jasper County, Illinois, 29
Jasper (dog), 67–68
Jefferson Elementary School, Enid, 19,
    111
John Jacobs Invitational, 51
Johnson, Bruce, 24
Johnson, Doc, 50
Johnston, Howard, 60

Kamm, Robert B., 27
Kansas City, Missouri, 22
Kansas Relays, 28, 39, 51
Kapyong Barracks, 46
Kenora, Ontario, 70
Kent Park, Montreal, 74
Kent Road School, Winnipeg, 68, 70–
    73, 97, 105–106, 109
Keogh, Mike, 87
Kilcona Park, Winnipeg, *ill*, 130, 133–
    134, 139
Kildonan Park, 106
Kimeto, Joshua, 84
KK (Katharine Chaney, niece), 137
Klassen, Darren, *ill*, 118–120, 133
Klassen, Henry, 98
Knapp, Ken, 24
Knights of Columbus Indoor Games, 84
Knoxville, Tennessee, 87, 98
Kooymans, Jerry, 104

Krushel, Rosemary, 71–72, 73
Kumar, Dr., 69, 81, 107, 130–131

La Barriere Park, 103, *ill*
Labatt's 20-km run, 104
Lake Tahoe, 52, *ill*
Laubert, Tom, 40
Laval, Quebec, 87
Lawrence, Kansas, 21, 22, 28, 39, *ill*
Lawson, John, 21, 22, 24, 25
Lawton, Oklahoma, 62, 63
Lee, Dennis, 71
Lewis Stadium Oval, 25
Lindgren, Gerry, 39
Little League Baseball, 18, 38
Little Tennessee River, 35–36
London Olympics, 98–99
Lord Roberts Community School,
    Winnipeg, 105
Lowe, Jim, 99, 100, 137

Mackintosh, Marie (first wife) *See*
    McCubbins, Marie
Mackintosh, Maudie (mother-in-law),
    67–68
Maggie Valley Moonlight Race, 116
Malaysia, 121
Manhattan, Kansas, 20
Manitoba Masters Swimming
    Championships, 104
Manitoba Runners' Association (MRA),
    award to CM, 15, 116
Manitoba Senior Cross Country
    Championships, 117
Manitoba Sports Hall of Fame, 48, *ill*,
    139–140
Manitoba Track & Field Association,
    CM's records, 97–98
Maple Grove Park, 117
Martin, Bill, Jr., 71
Martin, Ron, 84
Mashburn, Jim, 20
Maski-Courons race, 107
Mason, John, 39
Masters Class races, 107, 110, 112–117

McCollum, Dr., 37, 55–56
McCubbins, Chris:
  LIFE: father's family, 29–33; mother's
    family, 34–37; is born, 32; age at
    starting school, 19, 20–21, 128;
    grows up in Enid, 17–19, *ill*; stud-
    ies and runs at OSU, 19–28, *ill*;
    first visits Winnipeg, 45; relation-
    ship with Marie (first wife), 46,
    47–48, 50, 58–59, 62, 68; receives
    BSc, 52; first works with children
    during summer jobs, 68, 123; starts
    teaching, 68; applies for Canadian
    citizenship, 83; begins relationship
    with Sue (second wife), 100–101;
    moves to Victoria and back, 106–
    107; travels around Pacific Rim
    with Sue, 121–122; is diagnosed
    with leukemia, 15–16; marries Sue,
    81; dies, 138. *See also* Jacobsen, Sue
    (second wife)
  CHARACTER: "race face", 11; competi-
    tiveness, 13–14, 104; toughness, 13,
    27; principled approach, 14, 72; joy
    of running, 15, 39; introspective-
    ness, 19; confidence, 21; dedica-
    tion, 27; foresight, 27; work ethic,
    39–40, 60, 119, 120; mischievous
    smile, 41; creativity, 42; stamina
    and perseverance, 42; patriotism,
    54, 91; respect for parents' expecta-
    tions, 54; sportsmanship, 91; pride,
    92–93; gentleness, 100, 110; toler-
    ance, 101; is commended by prin-
    cipal, 106; modesty, 110; coaching
    expressive of, 120; nurturing dis-
    advantaged kids, 129–130; chooses
    the hard way, 133; reconnects with
    friends, 136, 137, 141
  ATTITUDES: pain in running, 15; draft
    dodging, 54; interested in psychol-
    ogy, 65–66, 68; likes Canada, 85;
    disappointed by his performance in
    Montreal, 93–94; Winnipeg win-
    ters, 105; curious about personality

types, 110; credo, 115; drug free, 115, 129; charitable giving, 122; gratitude, 131, 133, 137; living for the day, 140

FRIENDS: Gemmell, Greg, 14–15, 102, 103, 107, 116, 117; Fulton, Vic, 17–18; Smith, Ray, 19, 27, 50; Von Ruden, Tom, 23, 26, 28, 42, 45, *ill*; reconnects with, 136, 137, 141; Daly, Jim, 137; Lowe, Jim, 137. *See also* Reynolds, Sheldon; Sproll, Karl and Dianne; Towns, Grant

RECREATION: goes canoeing, *ill*, 136–137; dances like alligator, 42; sees *Hair* without Marie, 62; disco dancing, 71; goes camping, 72–73, *ill*; watches stage show with Sue, 101; plays crib, 108, 109; folk dancing, 109; watches movie, 109; keeps garden, 119; travels around Pacific Rim with Sue, 121–122

QUIRKS: appetite, 25–26, 100–101; dances like alligator, 42; dress sense, 47, *ill*; grooming, 64, 100; pancakes, 69, 73, 99, 119; takes lamb to school, 111

HEALTH: cardiovascular fitness, 9, 41–42, 125; tonsils, 18; back injury, 22; appetite, 25–26, 84, 101, 119; fall in Dusseldorf, 48–49; flu, 51, 97; groin injuries, 51, 87–90, 92, 94; neck dislocation and leg fracture, 53, 83; ulcer and neck pain, 61; Achilles tendon injury, 66; foot fracture, 78; tendon and calf pain, 79; Olympics exclusion and, 83–84; leg injury, 95; caution about injuries, 113; viral infection, 116; rest after injuries, 125

LEUKEMIA: is shocked by diagnosis, 15; begins chemotherapy, 16; "The New Adventure Begins" (cancer diary), 68–69, 80–82, 108–109, 140; achieves remissions, 81; hopes for stem cell transplant from siblings, 80–82; hopes Lenalinomide

will work, 108–109; receives antibiotics at Cancer Care, 127; reads *The Outliers* in hospital, 128–129; undergoes bone marrow aspiration, 130; tries to stay focused in face of bad news, 134; visits neighbour while smoke alarm beeps, 135; is transferred to palliative care, 131, 140; dies, 138

RUNNING: "race face", 11; in high school, 18–19, 38, *ill*; unathletic as late as tenth grade, 18, 128; effect of age at starting school, 20–21, 128; relay races, 22–25; track surfaces, 23, 45, 119; joy/love of, 39, 102, 139–140; is named track captain, 40; diary, 74, 77, 78, 79, 80, 84, 85, 86–91, 95, 96, 103, 104, 105, 117, 125, 126; sponsored shoes, 77–78; after bicycle thief, 95; list of races, 142–157

RUNNING, CROSS COUNTRY: 70, 78–79, 96–97, 104, 106–107, 117; in high school, 18, 19, 38; for OSU, 19–22, 26–27, *ill*; after altitude training, 43; pentathlon and, 57–58; for University of Manitoba, 64, 66, 67; coaching, 97, 109; trail at Kilcona Park, 133–134, 139

TRAINING: 89, 102–103; hard workouts, 14, 27–28, 42, 46, 52, 59, 73, 103, 115, 118–119; for Mexico Olympics, 40, 41, 43; on misconfigured treadmill, 42; in Montreal, 89–90; fartlek, 90; rest and, 125–126

RUNS BY DISTANCE: half-mile, 22, 38; 1500-metre, 98; one-mile, 19, 20, 21, 22, 25, 38, 39, 40; 3000-metre, 84, 98; 3000-metre steeplechase, 27, 28, 39–40, 41, 43, 45, 46–47, 48–49, 51, 52, *ill*, 60, 62, 64, 66, 73, 75, 76, 92, 98, 112; two-mile, 20, 22, 39, 50–52, *ill*; two-mile relay, 23; 4000-metre, 58, 78; 2.5-mile distance medley, 23–25;

three-mile, 20, 25, 26, 27, 39, 40, 41, 42, 43; 5000-metre, 60, 70, 73, 75, 85–86, 86, 86–87, 87, 98, 103; four-mile, 26; eight-km, 103, 116; 5.4-mile open road, 70; six-mile, 21; 10,000-metre, 39, 74, 75, 91, 98, 98–99, 103, 113; 10-km, 51, 70, 73, 85–86, 86, 86–87, 87, 106, 113, 114, 116, 117; 12,000-metre, 70, 78–79; 7.5-mile, 106–107; 15-km, 103, 113, 114–115, 117; 10-mile, 14–15, 103; one-hour, 77; 20-km, 107, 117; marathons, 42
RECORD-BREAKING RACES: ill, 158; OSU distance medley, 23; Ames cross country, 26–27; Big Eight and Kansas Relays, 39–40; NCAA steeplechase, 43, ill; Pan Am steeplechase, 46; Canadian and Manitoba native 10,000-metre, 74; Manitoba native records, 77, 97–98
RUNNING COMPETITORS FROM: University of Kansas, 22, 42; Kansas State University, 26, 42; Fort Hays State College, 39, ill; Washington State University, 39, 70; Minnesota, 42; Oregon, 42; Brigham Young University, 44; Australia, 50–51; Casa Grande, 52; Canadian Track & Field Association, 70; Ireland, 70; Ethopia, 75, 116; Ontario, 78; Kenya, 84, 117; United Kingdom, 84, 104, 113, 116; New York Athletic Club, 87; Toronto, 104; Germany, 113; Mexico, 116
AWARDS AND RECOGNITION: 9; Manitoba Runners' Association (MRA), 15, 116; Oklahoma State University, 26–27, 38, 41; All-American College Track and Field Team, 28; Manitoba Sports Hall of Fame, 48, ill, 139–140; Western Canada Summer Games gold medal, 75–76; Peter Gzowski, 91–92; cross country trails renamed in CM's honour, 133; kids' ski program renamed in CM's honour, 137
COACHING: boosting people's confidence, 15, 120, 129; for University of Manitoba, 65, 68, 97; cross country running, 97, 109; school sports, 109; steadfastly supports Klassen, 118–120
SKIING: Great Get Off Your Butt and Ski Program, ill, 130, 132, 139; with Sue, 15, 16; suspends trainer certification, 16; for workout, 103; kids' program renamed in CM's honour, 137
OTHER SPORTS: 102, 104; modern pentathlon, 56–63, 102; fencing, 58, 59; swimming, 58, 102, 104; equestrian competitions, 59
STUDIES: OSU, 19, 38, 50, 51, 52, 65; University of Manitoba, 61, 65–66, 68, 95–96, 97; University of California, 95–96
TEACHING: early childhood education, 68, 95–96, 105; is hired by Winnipeg School Division, 68; Kent Road School, 68, 70–73, 97, 105–106, 109; holds dance classes, 71; presents "Noodles" toque, 71; uses time-outs, 71, 124; skilfully meets students' special needs, 72, 105; evaluation of, 97, 105–106; organizes dance events, 109; relationship with students, 109, 110, 111, 139–140; Riverview School Kindergarten, 109–111; David Livingstone School, 123–124, 129; computer training, 129–130, 139–140
McCubbins, Churchill (great-grand-father), 29–30, ill
McCubbins, Clarence Ferns (father), 31–33, 43, ill, 59, ill
McCubbins, Clarence Raymond "Wild Cat Ferns" (grandfather), 30–31, ill
McCubbins, Juanita (née Snider) (mother), 18, 22, 32–33, 43, ill, 54, 59, 69,·

ill; supports CM during illness, 132, 138

McCubbins, Lillie May (great-grand-mother), 30, *ill*

McCubbins, Marie (first wife), 46, 47–48, 50, 58–59, 62, 68, *ill*

McCubbins, Philip Winston "Win" (brother), 32, 43, *ill*, 56, 81, *ill*; supports CM during illness, 81, 132, 135, 137

McCubbins, Raymond Chris *See* McCubbins, Chris

McCubbins, Rilla (sister) *See* Chaney, Rilla

McCubbins, Robert Raymond (uncle), 31

McCubbins, Steffie (Stephanie H. McCubbins, sister-in-law), 137–138

McCubbins, Tipton "Tip" F. (brother), 18–19, 26, 28, 32, *ill*, 58, *ill*; supports CM during illness, 80–81, 107–108, 135, 137–138; helps CM find niche, 128

McCubbins, Zach Hilton (great-great-grandfather), 29, *ill*

McKay, Bruce, 118

McLaren, Grant, 78–79

McVickar, Scotty (trainer, a.k.a. "Dr."), 79, 88

Meadowlands Park, New Jersey, 107

Mendoza, Ed, 86

Mercier Tables, 98

Metcalf, Jim, 19, 20–21, 23, *ill*, 128

Mexico City Olympics, 40, 41, 43, 44

Mielke, Guenter, 113

Minneapolis, Minnesota, 45

Missouri-OSU meet, 38

modern pentathlon, 56–63, 102

Monmouth County, New Jersey, 114

Monroe, Louisiana, 52

Montreal, Quebec, 47–48, 74, 98; Olympic Games, 68, 75, 89–94

Moody, Bob, *ill*

Moore, Oscar, 52

Morningside, 91–93

Muirhead, Iris, 110

Muncy, Alma (grandmother), 31

Murphy, Jim, 51

National Collegiate Athletic Association (NCAA), 21, 22, 28, 39, *ill*

Nelson, Van, 45

New Zealand, 122

Ngeno, John, 70

Nightingale, Conrad, 23, 26, 42, 43, 45, 46–47, 48–49, 51, *ill*, 66

Norman, Oklahoma, 40, 41, 51

Ogden, Glen, 39

Oklahoma State University (OSU): athletics, 19–28, 38–41, 43, 44–45, 50, *ill*, 85; financial support from, 19, 20; studies, 19, 38, 50, 51, 52, 65; recognition by, 26–27, 38, 41; father scrimps to attend, 32

Oksana (health worker), 68

Olsen, Larry, 116

Olympic Games: Higgins' coaching for, 20; US trials, 40, 52–53; Alamosa runners, 42–43, *ill*, 125–126; Mexico City (1968), 44, 83; CM's ambitions, 52, 66, 83; training at Lake Tahoe, 52; modern pentathlon in, 57–58; Munich (1972), 66, 83; Canadian trials, 66, 74, 87; Montreal (1976), 68, 75, 89–94; Moscow (1980), 75; London (2012) 10,000-metre times, 98–99; Barcelona (1992) as Klassen goal, 118

O'Riordan, T., 60

Pan American Games, 43, 45, 64

Pan American Stadium, Winnipeg, 73, 106

pentathlon, 56–63, 102

Perry, David, 23

Perry, John, 23

Perry, Oklahoma, 29, 30, 31

Perth, Australia, 122

Phil (Sue's pastor), 81, 137

Photosprint, 45

pistol shooting, 58
Pokes (OSU team, a.k.a. Cowboys), 20, 23, 24
Portland, Oregon, 113, 114
Prairie 12,000-metre Cross Country Championships, 96
Price, Bob, 48
Provo, Utah, 43
Puma series, 106, 116, 117

"race face", 11
Rae & Jerry's Steak House, 47
Red Rock, Oklahoma, 31
Regina, Saskatchewan, 75
relay races, 22–25
Remple, Wally, 102
Reynolds, Sheldon: at tree planting, *ill*; on CM's psychological sharpness, 14; first works out with CM, 65; competes in Kenora, 70; on CM's running style, 73; on CM's mid-race power, 75; running times, 76; cools down with CM in Sudbury, 77; on CM's Montreal disappointment, 93–94; on CM's records, 98; trains with CM, 103, *ill*; on CM's competitiveness, 104; on CM's rest practices, 126; walks with CM during illness, 135
Richards, Bob, 44
Riley, Mavis, 70, 72
Riley, Stephen, 108–109, 136
Riverview School, Winnipeg, 109–111
Rodgers, Bill, 116
Roelants, Gaston, 47
Rogers, Arkansas, 29
Rono, Henry, 114
Ross, George (uncle), 18
Ross, Hope Snider (aunt), 18, 32
Rubinger, Dr., 82
Run for Fun, 102, 103, 116
Runner's World, 113, 116
Ryun, Jim, 25, 42

San Anselmo, California, 85, 121
San Antonio, Texas, 58

Santa Monica, California, 26
Sargent Park Pool, 100, 102
Saskatchewan Centennial Indoor Games, 50
Saskatoon, Saskatchewan, 50–51, 79–80, 96
Schwitzer, David, 81
Scotland, 96
Scott, George, 50
Seagren, Bob, 45
Seattle, Washington, 66, 98
Senior Canadian Championships, 66
Sensory Integration and Learning Disorders, 95–96
SERVAS, 122
Sheppard Inter-Service Track & Field Championships, 60
Shorter, Grant, 116
Simon, Jay, 23–24
Singapore, 121
Smith, Ray, 19, 27, 50, *ill*
Snider, Edwin "Ed" (uncle), 34–37
Snider, Henry Tipton (grandfather), 34
Snider, Juanita (mother) *See* McCubbins, Juanita
Snider, Nathan Hale (mother's cousin), 55–56
Soulsby, Bruce, 99, 102, *ill*
Spokane, Washington, 107
Sproll, Dianne, 13, 133
Sproll, Karl: at tree planting, *ill*; on CM mentoring runners at U of M, 65; running partner, 70, 103, *ill*; on CM strategizing for the one-hour race, 77; CM ill in Vancouver with, 78–79; supports CM during illness, 133
St. Boniface Hospital, 16
St. Catharines, Ontario, 70
St-Gabriel-de-Brandon, Quebec, 107
St. Louis, Missouri, 63
St. Vital Park, 106
Stanley Park, Vancouver, 78–79
steeplechase, 27–28, 39–41, 43, 44–49, 51, 52, *ill*, 60, 62, 64, 75, 76

Stillwater, Oklahoma, 19, 20, 25, 26, 52
Sudbury, Ontario, 76–77
Superior, Arizona, 31
Swanson, Gary, *ill*
Switzer, Larry, 70

Tellico River, 35, 36
Texas Relays, 23–25, 40
Thailand, 121
The Outliers, 128
3M Company, 45
Tipton, Henry, 34
Tom Black Classic meet, 87
Toronto, Ontario, 66
Towns, Grant, 76, 115; at tree planting, *ill*; initial judgment of CM's running, 46; brings food during CM's illness, 69; on CM's toughness on bad tracks, 96; Yellow Snow Club, 99, *ill*; on CM's hard workouts, 103
Traynor, Pat, 45, 47, 48
Triangular Meet, 39
Tulsa, Oklahoma, 54

Ulla Jean (littler child), 18
University of California, distance education, 95–96
University of Kansas, 21, 22
University of Manitoba: athletics, 61, 64–65, 68, 97; psychology studies, 61, 65–66, 68; education studies, 68, 95–96, 97
University of Manitoba Stadium, 66, 113
University of Minnesota, 41, 45
University of Oklahoma, 25
US Air Force, 45, 47
US Army: athletics, 41, 56, *ill*; draft, 55; transfer to reserve, 63; discharge, 160
US Army Reserves, 63
US Modern Pentathlon Training Center, 58
US Olympic Team, 20, 42–43, 125–126

Van der Wal, Hylke, 28, 39
Vancouver, B.C., 78–79

Viareggio, Italy, 49
Victoria, British Columbia, 15–16, 104–105, 106–107
Victoria Cross Country Trials, 104
Vietnam War, 54, 57, 59
Villanueva, Antonio, 114, 115, 116
Von Ruden, Tom, 23, 26, 28, 42, 45, *ill*
Von Troba, Al, 24
Vonore, Tennessee, 33, 55

Waigwa, Wilson, 117
Walker, Bob, 102
Webber, Chris, 98
Western Canada Game Trials, 115
Western Canada Summer Games, 75
Wichita Falls, Texas, 60
Windsor Park Nordic Centre, Winnipeg, *ill*, 132
Winnipeg Beach, 116
Winnipeg Free Press, 50–51, 75–76, 83–84, 97, 112–113, 117, 139–140
Winnipeg, Manitoba: pizza promotion, 26; CM's first visit, 45; runs in and around, 46–47, 66, 78, 84, 98, 103, 106, 113, 116, 117; visits Marie's family, 50; visit after Lake Tahoe, 53; draft and, 54; return before Montreal Olympics, 88; return to, 107
Winnipeg School Division: hired by, 68; time off, 84, 96; returns to, 109
Winnipeg Tribune, 102
World Cross Country Championship, 107

Yaleville, Illinois, 29
Yellow Snow Track Club, 46, 83, 99, 100, 104, *ill*, 116, 118, 132
Yifter, Miruts "the Shifter", 73–74, 73–75
Young, George, 52